# SPARKLING FACETS:

# BIBLE NAMES AND TITLES OF JESUS

## COMPILED BY HAYES PRESS

Copyright © Hayes Press 2015

All rights reserved. No part of this book may be reproduced, stored in a retrieval system, or transmitted in any form, without the written permission of Hayes Press.

Published by:

**HAYES PRESS Publisher, Resources & Media**

The Barn, Flaxlands

Royal Wootton Bassett

Swindon, SN4 8DY

United Kingdom

www.hayespress.org

Unless otherwise indicated, all Scripture quotations are from the HOLY BIBLE, the Revised Version (Public Domain). Scriptures marked NIV are from New International Version®, NIV® Copyright © 1973, 1978, 1984, 2011 by Biblica, Inc.™ Used by permission. All rights reserved worldwide.

# CHAPTER ONE: INTRODUCTION (JOHN TERRELL)

In this book, we are making a study of the names and titles of the Lord Jesus Christ in the Bible. Those who love and aspire to serve the Saviour can easily identify with Paul when he wrote to the Philippians, 'I also count all things loss for the excellence of the knowledge of Christ Jesus my Lord', continuing with the words, "that I may gain Christ, and again, that I may know Him and the power of His resurrection" (Philippians 3:8,10).

One of the ways in which we can enhance our knowledge of Him is through an understanding of His names and titles. It was David, another great man of God, who expressed himself in sublime poetry in Psalm 8: "O, LORD, our Lord, How excellent is Your name in all the earth, Who set Your glory above the heavens!" Jesus Himself said, "Learn from Me," and He promised rest of soul to those who do. We shall learn about Him by examining the divine Name in some of its lovely and expressive forms. His is indeed an excellent Name and Paul strongly encouraged the Philippian church of God to "approve the things that are excellent" (Philippians 1:10).

In the book of Proverbs, there are many wide-ranging, wise sentiments and poetic statements about the Person and ways of God. Some are called 'oracles' or 'utterances' and they are placed there by the Holy Spirit for our meditation and enlightenment. One very interesting one is in Proverbs chapter 30, where a wise man called Agur declares to his friends: "Surely I am more stupid than any man, and do not have the understanding of a man. I neither learned wisdom nor have knowledge of the Holy One". That was a very honest and candid confession of his own limitations! Then he goes on: "Who has ascended into heaven, or descended? Who has gathered the wind in His fists? Who has bound the waters in a garment? Who has established all the ends of the earth? What is His name, and what is His Son's name, if you know?"

And Agur adds further wise words beginning with, "Every word of God is pure". Don't the words, "Who has gathered the wind in His fists?" immediately carry us in thought to a raging tempest on the Sea of Galilee? Can't we hear again the calm, majestic command of Deity, "Peace, be still!" and share again the awe and amazement of the fishermen of the lake as they whispered among themselves, "Who can this be, that even the wind and the sea obey Him!" Agur, the wise man of Proverbs said, "What is His name, and what is His Son's name, if you know?"

If the disciples were in any doubt about this, that doubt didn't last long. As soon as their fishing boat reached the shore they had the answer, and from a most unexpected source. Two demon-possessed men came screaming down the hillside crying out, "What have we to do with You, Jesus ... the Holy One of God!" The Master rebuked the demons, but not for calling Him by the wrong name. For, as the epistle of James declares, "Even the demons believe - and tremble!" (2:19). "What is His Son's name?" asked Agur.

Some of the names of the Lord Jesus in the Bible are names or titles that God His Father gave Him, or will yet give Him in the future. The precious name 'Jesus' was decreed by the Father to Joseph - who was to be the head of the Nazareth family into which the Lord was virgin-born. The title 'Servant' was also given by God to His Son in the prophetic scriptures. "Behold! My Servant ..." (Isaiah 42:1). And. looking into the future, in the book of Revelation we are told that the glorious Person on the white horse is called "Faithful and True and KING OF KINGS AND LORD OF LORDS"; and in addition, He has a name written that no-one knows but Himself (Revelation 19:11-16).

Then again, some of the Lord's designations were given to Him by others. To John, the remarkable forerunner of the Christ, it was given to apply that title which has come to mean so much to all His own, and to encapsulate the wonder of His redemptive work, namely "Lamb of God". That is one name we shall be looking at if we are to feel the power of its gentle and sacrificial message. And we remember how the Lord Jesus challenged the rich young man who approached Him with the words, "Good Teacher, what shall I do that I may inherit eternal life?" He was not wrong in calling Jesus 'good', but he didn't understand the true and profound significance of his words. Don't we also all too often speak of the Lord in terms of His truly wonderful names and titles but with scant appreciation of their truly deep and eternal meaning? Perhaps our study together will help us in that regard.

Of outstanding importance, too, are some of the names that the Lord Jesus gave Himself. Some of the most wonderful of these are in the book of Revelation. "I am the Alpha and the Omega" (Revelation 1:8); "I am the Root and the Offspring of David, the Bright and Morning Star" (Revelation 22:16) to mention but two. And, of course, in the Gospel according to John, the Lord joins to His supreme 'I Am' title a very special series of designations, including, "I am the bread of life"; "I am the door"; "I am the vine" - and others. Yet perhaps one of the loveliest, if not the most immediately arresting, is the title by which the Lord refers to Himself in the gospels, "Son of Man". This is another we must examine, for it's expressive of so much that concerns the eternal counsels of God in salvation. It sums up so much that's involved in the incarnation of the Son of God and His amazing eternal identification with us in our humanity. So we have a wide canvas to paint and we'll by no means be able to cover it all; but if we can share some of the richness of the colour and form of the names and titles of our Lord, we will surely derive great benefit and spiritual uplift together.

# CHAPTER TWO: SON OF GOD (JOHN TERRELL)

In this chapter, we will consider briefly the title 'Son of God' as applied in the New Testament to the Lord Jesus Christ. Of all the designations of our Lord, this is surely the most basic and the most significant in relation to His character and Person. The golden words of John 3:16 are loved and treasured in every Christian's experience: "For God so loved the world that He gave His only begotten Son, that whoever believes in Him should not perish but have everlasting life."

In the same way, we love to echo the words of Paul in our own hearts when he spoke in deep devotion of "the Son of God, who loved me and gave Himself for me" (Galatians 2:20). John 3:16 establishes the universal saving love of the Godhead centred in the only begotten Son of God; and Paul's words in Galatians speak of the sacrificial love of the Son in an intensely personal way.

The name 'Son of God' was pronounced by God through the spokesmanship of the angel Gabriel to Mary at the annunciation. The words were unmistakable and direct, "that Holy One who is to be born will be called the Son of God" (Luke 1:35); the divine identity of the 'Holy One' was spelled out to Mary. Her son was the Son of God. Men and even demons later confessed Him to be the Son of God, but God declared it in the clearest and most definite terms even before His birth.

Then by Jordan's banks there came these words from heaven, "You are My beloved Son; in You I am well pleased". And it was the eternal Sonship to which this testimony was given, for the eternal character of His Sonship is vital in Christian doctrine. "God gave His only begotten Son and the Father ... sent the Son as Savior of the world". It requires distortion of the ordinary sense of these words to suggest that the One given and sent was not the Son of the Father before His incarnation. Many other scriptures attest the same point.

Returning now to the rich tapestry of witness to the divine Sonship of Jesus, starting as we have done from the testimony of the Father and Son themselves, we find that the range of acknowledgement is remarkably wide; and all of this in the context of the profound meaning of the title in contemporary Jewish thought and theology. The Jewish leaders knew beyond all doubt the exact significance of the Lord's claim to be the Son of God. When He declared, "My Father has been working until now, and I have been working", we read that: "... the Jews sought all the more to kill Him, because He not only broke the Sabbath, but also said that God was His Father, making Himself equal with God" (John 5:17,18).

Sceptics of our own day may dispute the issue, but not the religious Jews then! Furthermore, the adversary and his demons knew all about it. The demons of Gadara openly declared Jesus to be the Son of God; and in the wilderness temptation of our Lord after His baptism Satan betrayed the same knowledge: "If You are the Son of God, command that these stones become bread ... throw Yourself down" (Matthew 4:3,6). We hear the same malignant tones in the voices of those who challenged the Lord Jesus on the cross. "If you are the Son of God, come down from the cross" (Matthew 27:40).

Now Jesus knew well that a conviction about His divine Sonship was vital, above all others, for those men He was preparing to carry forward the gospel story into all the world after His death and resurrection. So their journey of understanding to the point of assurance and certainty was particularly important. Aside from the remarkable early acknowledgement by Nathaniel, "Rabbi, You are the Son of God!" (John 1:49), for the disciples as a whole, a settled conviction about the divine Sonship of their Master came more slowly. In the storm on the lake they asked, "Who can this be, that even the winds and the sea obey Him?" (Matthew 8:26,27). Later in the episode of His appearance walking on the water, they were ready to exclaim, "Truly You are the Son of God" (Matthew 14:33). Doubtless this marked an important stage in their understanding of their Master's true identity.

But the time was near when the Lord must draw from His men a clearly considered declaration of their absolute assurance about His divine Person. This He did at Caesarea Philippi. In that quiet retreat, He led them to the ultimate challenge, "Who do you say that I am?' Simon Peter answered and said, 'You are the Christ, the Son of the living God".

Without doubt this was a defining moment in the spiritual experience of His disciples that the Lord had been leading them to. The Lord responded to Peter's confession of faith with the solemn declaration, "Blessed are you, Simon Bar-Jonah, for flesh and blood has not revealed this to you, but My Father who is in heaven". One of those disciples was, of course, John son of Zebedee. To him it was given by the Holy Spirit to record, more than any other New Testament writer, the profound things of the One called 'Son of God'. It is he who gives us the very important qualifying word 'only begotten' in connection with the Son; a matter of deep significance which, amongst other important things, marks out the absolute uniqueness of the Sonship of the Lord Jesus Christ.

We have already seen the words 'only begotten' in John 3:16 and they occur also in chapter 1 vv.14 and 18. In the latter verse He is the "only begotten Son, who is in the bosom of the Father" - an expression of profound truth too deep for us to fully fathom, yet so clearly indicating a unique nearness to, and identity of relationship with, the Father. And as the ageing John closed his gospel record he could declare: "these are written that you may believe that Jesus is the Christ, the Son of God, and that believing you may have life in His name" (John 20:31).

The beloved disciple is taken up with the same sublime truths in his epistles culminating in the final chapter of 1 John where we have the ringing confirmation of the closing words of his gospel: "He who has the Son has life; he who does not have the Son of God does not have life. These things I have written to you who believe in the name of the Son of God, that you may know that you have eternal life" (1 John 5:12,13). On such a confident, triumphant note, we must leave our brief reflections on the wonderful name and title 'Son of God'. All that Scripture has to say about it instructs our minds and hearts about our glorious Saviour. And at the same time, it draws us very near in loving adoration to the One whom Paul learned to revere and serve as 'the Son of God who loved me and gave Himself for me'.

"Jesus, the Son of God

Bore sin's accursed load,

Praise to His name.

Sing, we who know his blood

Hath brought us night to God,

And crowned us with all good,

Worthy His name."

(J. Allen)

# CHAPTER THREE: SON OF MAN (JOHN TERRELL)

One of the most important and widely applied titles of the Lord Jesus is Son of Man. "Who," the Master asked His disciples, "do men say that I, the Son of Man, am?" The very question pin-points the fact that the Lord had come to be widely known by that name, at least among His disciples. For it was the name He gave Himself. We saw, when examining the title Son of God, that it was primarily awarded by the Father to the Son - right from the annunciation of His birth. But the title Son of Man was the one assumed by the Lord Himself. It was in this way that He referred to Himself in the third person, clearly conveying a message about His person, work and destiny. Why should this have been, and what can we learn about the Lord and His purposes from it?

Now 'bar nasha', the Aramaic 'son of man' was not normally used as any kind of title. It was simply the usual expression for a man, a human being. And the Lord Jesus ordinarily spoke in Aramaic. So was the Lord's only objective in assuming Son of Man as a name for Himself to underline His humanity; indeed to separate that from His parallel claim to deity? Some have thought so, but this really is not an adequate answer.

The very question quoted above, as posed by the Lord to His disciples, and the following challenge to them, "but who do you say that I am?" - had the very purpose of identifying the Son of Man and the Son of God as one and the same Person. Not that the title Son of Man does not, in many of its occurrences, remind us very powerfully of the true and perfect humanity of our Lord; for example where one of the Old Testament uses of the term is applied to Christ. In Hebrews chapter 2 verses 6-8 the words of Psalm 8 are quoted:

"What is man that You are mindful of him, or the son of man that You visit him? For You have made him a little lower than the angels, and You have crowned him with glory and honour. You have made him to have dominion over the works of Your hands. You have put all things under his feet."

There can be no doubt that this psalm has a double application - to Adam and his descendants, and also to the Lord Jesus. In the latter case, it does indeed focus on His incarnation and humanity. But the title Son of Man, as assumed and used by the Lord while on earth, surely carries us back to the prophecy of Daniel. In chapter 7 of that book we have depicted fearsome animals believed by many to represent world powers which would dominate human history. Then a day of divine judgement comes, presided over by One called 'the Ancient of Days'. And as Daniel watched he exclaimed: "And behold, One like the Son of Man, coming with the clouds of heaven ... to Him was given dominion and glory and a kingdom."

So, in Jewish religious thinking down the years, there was an expectation of a Messianic Deliverer who would answer to Daniel's vision, a conquering victorious champion, 'Son of Man'. Victorious and powerful as He would be, He also stood in contrast, in terms of humanity and justice, with the cruel, ruthless character of the beasts portrayed in the early verses of Daniel chapter 7. It was surely with all of this in mind that Jesus adopted this designation for Himself as the principal title of 'the days of His flesh'. Although the people to whom Christ spoke, as recorded in John chapter 12, scornfully asked the question, "Who is this Son of Man?", Jews who were knowledgeable in their religion and in the books of the law and the prophets, would readily associate 'Son of Man' with Daniel's prophecy.

Yet the Lord had to convey, especially to His disciples, that the title Son of Man was more comprehensive in its meaning than a study of the Daniel reference alone might suggest. It was only when the crisis confession at Caesarea Philippi was drawn from the disciples, "You (the Son of Man) are the Christ, the Son of the living God," that the Master began to seriously instruct them about His impending suffering, death and resurrection. "The Son of Man must suffer many things," He said. Peter's immediate reaction, we remember, was to repudiate the whole idea of suffering, drawing from the Lord the very severe rebuke, "Get behind Me, Satan."

The old adversary of the wilderness temptations spoke through the lips of the Lord's own disciple to try to deflect the Lord from the way of suffering. For when He spoke of Himself as the Son of Man, He did so in terms of the whole scope of His redemptive purpose in coming into the world.

Beginning early on with reference to His alienation from human comforts and achievement, "Foxes have holes," He said, "and birds of the air have nests, but the Son of Man has nowhere to lay His head" (Luke 9:58), the Lord went on to relate His Son of Man character to all His greatest claims and declarations about Himself. Notable are the words, "The Son of Man has come to seek and to save that which was lost;" and again, "For even the Son of Man did not come to be served, but to serve, and to give His life a ransom for many." And in response to the contemptuous unbelief of the scribes recorded in Mark chapter 2, who accused Him of blasphemy for conferring forgiveness of sins, the Master said, "That you may know that the Son of Man has power on earth to forgive sins ... Arise, take up your bed." More directly, however, the Lord spoke to His disciples at Caesarea Philippi of the suffering and death that must befall the Son of Man, as we have seen.

Yet the message of Daniel chapter 7 also must have its glorious fulfilment, and so we have very prominently presented in the Lord's teaching on future events, the triumphant and glorious advent of the Son of

Man in power and great glory (Matthew 24:30). We meditate on the Son of Man 'lifted up' at Calvary, as He Himself predicted, and look to the future of His universal exaltation at the winding up of this world's history.

After Stephen's dramatic declaration in Acts 7:56, "I see the heavens opened and the Son of Man standing at the right hand of God!" there is no further mention of the title Son of Man in the New Testament until we come to the end-time prophecies of the book of Revelation. Why should this be? Well, much that we have already noted has led many to feel that there is a special connection between the title 'Son of Man' and the spiritual fortunes of the nation of Israel. 'Son of Man' is undoubtedly a Messianic title, as our allusions to Daniel show. Today, while Israel nationally is set aside in God's purposes (as expounded by Paul in the Romans epistle), the Lord Jesus is building His Church, His Body. We live in 'the times of the Gentiles' and when 'the fulness of the Gentiles' arrives, then for Israel, "The Deliverer will come out of Zion, and He will turn away ungodliness from Jacob" (Romans 11:25-26). This can surely only relate to the Lord's prophecy in Matthew 24:30: "They will see the Son of Man coming on the clouds of heaven with power and great glory." Yet all this flows from the suffering of Calvary, for "They will look on Me whom they have pierced," as the prophet Zechariah said. We close our consideration of the divine Son of Man with the lovely words of a hymn of His sufferings:

"Stricken, smitten and afflicted,

Lo, He dies upon the tree;

'Tis the Christ by Man rejected

Son of God, 'tis He, 'tis He.

Mark the sacrifice appointed,

See who bears the awful load;

'Tis the Word, the Lord's Anointed,

Son of Man and Son of God!"

(T. Kelly)

# CHAPTER FOUR: SON OF DAVID (JOHN TERRELL)

Having considered the titles 'Son of God' and 'Son of Man', we now come to a very interesting title of the Lord's Sonship, namely, 'Son of David'. If, as we saw, the name Son of God was outstandingly God's name for His Son; and Son of Man the Lord's name for Himself, then Son of David was predominantly the Jews' name for Jesus. Not that the title was first applied in Scripture by the Jewish people of His day. Indeed, His lineage through David was specified as clearly at the annunciation by the angel Gabriel as was the name Son of God. Gabriel said to Mary "He will be great, and will be called the Son of the Highest; and the Lord God will give Him the throne of His father David".

When Matthew came in due course to write his gospel narrative, he opened it with, "The book of the genealogy of Jesus Christ, the Son of David". Still, it is usually from the lips of the Jewish people with whom the Lord Jesus came in contact, that we have Him described as 'Son of David'. We can easily forget what a heroic figure of history King David was to the Jews. So much so that, after the sacking of Jerusalem in A.D. 70, two Roman emperors, fearful of a resurgence of Jewish nationalism, ordered the destruction of all direct descendants of David - shades of the slaughter of the innocents by Herod at the time of the Lord's nativity.

It was during the first century before His birth that Jewish poets first directly called the expected Messiah, Son of David. So the linkage of this title with the anticipated Messiah was already established in Jewish thought when the Lord Jesus came among them. On the last great day of the Feast of Tabernacles, as recounted in John chapter 7, some people out of the crowd said, "Has not the Scripture said that the Christ comes from the seed of David and from the town of Bethlehem, where David was?" (John 7:42).

Furthermore, the writings of the ancient Hebrew prophets, linking Messiah to the family of David, were familiar to educated Jews. Jeremiah spoke of the Lord raising up a righteous Branch for David, and of David never lacking a man to sit on the throne of the house of Israel (Jeremiah 23:5; 33:17). So did Amos, Ezekiel and Zechariah, while Hosea spoke of the day when Israel would return and 'seek the Lord their God and David their king' (Hosea 3:5). But it is Isaiah who provides perhaps the most striking prophecy in chapter 9 verses 6, 7. There we have the Messianic prediction of the Child born and the Son given. "And the government will be upon His shoulder ... of the increase of His government and peace there will be no end, upon the throne of David and over His kingdom". But the extent to which the Jewish people of His own day perceived Him as the Son of David, is shown by the way many who were healed spoke of Him.

In Matthew 9:27-28, we read of two blind men who followed Jesus crying out, "Son of David, have mercy on us!" What is even more surprising and gratifying is the response of the men when the Lord challenged, "Do you believe that I am able to do this?" "Yes, Lord," was their short, direct answer, adding to their understanding of His Messiahship, faith in His divine authority as Lord. Little wonder that the Master immediately touched their eyes saying, "According to your faith let it be to you". A very similar occasion recurred later outside Jericho with two blind men addressing the Lord in identical terms and receiving the same desired blessing (Matthew 20:29-34). Another individual, who acknowledged Christ as Son of David, was the Syro-Phoenician woman whose daughter was healed. Again, her address was, "O Lord, Son of David" (Matthew 15:22), recognising the Messianic significance of the Name.

Then there was wider discussion of the matter when a blind and mute man was restored. We read, "And all the multitudes were amazed and said, "Could this be the Son of David?'" (Matthew 12:23). And when the time came for the triumphal entry into Jerusalem in fulfilment of the prophecy of Zechariah 9, "Then the multitudes who went before and those who followed cried out saying: "Hosanna to the Son of David! 'Blessed is He who comes in the name of the Lord!' Hosanna in the highest!'"

This, we read, was repeated in the Temple. How gratifying it must have been for the Lord Jesus to hear such acknowledgement by the common people who heard Him gladly. And how sad that their voice of praise was so soon to be silenced, and drowned by shouts of, 'Crucify!'

# CHAPTER FIVE: LAMB OF GOD
# (JOHN TERRELL)

Among the titles of the Lord Jesus in the Scriptures, 'Lamb of God' is perhaps the one which draws us in the deepest tenderness to Calvary and its amazing sacrifice. It brings flooding back so much of the Old Testament imagery of sacrifice and offerings which, over so many centuries of Israel's history, foreshadowed the coming of the Christ and His work of atonement and redemption. It floods with light the sacred message of Israel's central annual festival, the Passover, with all its association of divine delivering power flowing out of death and blood-shedding. It evokes the person of the Saviour in a beauty, humility and grace which quietens the spirit to meditation and worship.

"Behold! The Lamb of God who takes away the sin of the world!" The words were, of course, those of John on Jordan's banks; words which have inspired Christian thought and instructed devout minds over the centuries, concerning the saving purpose of the Son of God. At the very outset of the Lord's public ministry, these were the words to focus attention immediately on the very heart of His resolve in coming into the world, to go to Calvary 'for us men and for our salvation' as the fine words of the Catechism put it.

John first pointed Jesus out in these terms when he saw Him coming toward Him; and then later he again said, "Behold the Lamb of God!" and we also read he was 'looking at Jesus as He walked' (John 1:36). He came as the Lamb of God, and He walked this sad world as the Lamb of God. The lovely characteristics of meekness, innocence, humility, and submission to His Father's will, which attach to this precious title, were evident daily in His life and ministry. They delighted the Father hour by hour as Father and Son walked together to Calvary.

The vivid picture springs to mind of Abraham and Isaac who went together to Moriah. Then from Isaac came the burning question, "Look, the fire and the wood, but where is the lamb for a burnt offering?" And Abraham said, "My son, God will provide for Himself the lamb for a burnt offering." But no such question came from the Lamb of God, described in Revelation 13:8 as 'the Lamb slain from the foundation of the world'. Together Father and Son went to Calvary, in the complete understanding of the sacrifice ahead, and in full appreciation of the prophetic import of Isaiah's sombre words, 'He was led as a lamb to the slaughter, and as a sheep before its shearers is silent'. And it was while speaking of the unbroken communion of Father and Son in Matthew 11 – "No one knows the Son except the Father" - that the Lord gave us such precious words as, "I am gentle and lowly in heart."

As year succeeded year and century succeeded century, the morning and evening lamb was killed in the tabernacle or temple by the priests of Israel. Never did the sun rise and never did it set on planet earth but God saw Calvary portrayed before Him in all its awfulness and beauty, day in, day out. The people, even the priests, must often have slipped into something of a routine about it all, but not the God of heaven who loved His people Israel with an everlasting love; who "gave His only begotten Son, that whoever believes in Him should not perish but have everlasting life."

There were many occasions in Israel's calendar when lambs, as well as other animals, were sacrificed and all carried their prophetic message of the coming Christ. Outstanding, however, was the Passover. The hand of God was about to be revealed in overwhelming authority and power in delivering His people from Egypt. All of this could have been accomplished without sacrifice or the shedding of blood by the direct exercise of divine strength. But in the deeper purposes of God, deliverance from Egyptian bondage with all its overtones of sin and iniquity must be combined with divine judgement on that sin. And this meant a provision for the protection of His believing and faithful people.

So through Moses and Aaron came the command, "Speak to all the congregation of Israel saying, 'On the tenth day of this month every man shall take for himself a lamb, according to the house of his father, a lamb for a household." The rest of the story of that unforgettable night will be familiar to readers. The lamb selected, kept and scrutinised for flaws; its blood shed and placed on the lintel and posts of the doors; its flesh eaten roast with fire, unleavened bread and bitter herbs. So the memorial went on year after year until at last, at Calvary, the Lamb of God was slain, to the very hour, as the Passover lambs were being slaughtered in the temple courts.

The awfulness of sin, and the dreadful price of its cleansing, were uppermost in Paul's mind when he wrote to the Corinthians, 'Christ, our Passover, was sacrificed for us' (1 Corinthians 5:7). The disciple who was able to describe himself as a witness of the sufferings of Christ also wrote to the scattered Jewish Christians, 'knowing that you were not redeemed with corruptible things, like silver or gold ... but with the precious blood of Christ, as of a lamb without blemish and without spot.'

Down the now notorious Gaza Strip, a fine chariot rumbled its way south from Jerusalem. Its distinguished occupant, returning to Ethiopia, was in sombre mood, doubtless a disappointed and perplexed man. Jerusalem had failed to yield the spiritual secret he was searching for. But he had acquired a scroll of the prophet Isaiah. So he read, "He was led as a sheep to the slaughter, and as a lamb before its shearer is silent, so He opened not His mouth. In His humiliation His justice was taken away. And who will declare His generation? For His life is taken from the earth" (Acts 8:32,33). It was the old, ever new story of the seeking soul and the seeking Saviour. For Philip, the Lord's messenger in the Lord's message, welcomed the Ethiopian's response to his offer of help, and sitting alongside him in the chariot, he opened his mouth and, beginning at this Scripture, preached Jesus to him. We can hardly imagine that he did not tell him about the Baptist's cry, "Behold the Lamb of God!"

The New Testament book which speaks most of the Lord Jesus as the Lamb is, of course, the Revelation given to John. Transported to the throne room of heaven and the wonders of the living creatures and the elders, John looked and 'behold, in the midst of the throne and of the four living creatures, and in the midst of the elders, stood a Lamb as though it had been slain.'

Among nearly thirty references to Christ as the Lamb in Revelation, is the resounding hymn of adoration of ten thousand times ten thousand, and thousands of thousands of celestial beings, "Worthy is the Lamb who was slain to receive power and riches and wisdom, and strength and honor and glory and blessing!" Furthermore, we read that every created thing which is in the heaven, and on the earth, and under the earth, takes up the adoring cry, "Blessing and honor and glory and power be to Him who sits on the throne, and to the Lamb, forever and ever!" (Revelation 5:13). One day, praise God, our voices will join that great chorus of heavenly praise.

Spotless Lamb by God provided!

Here upon His face we gaze,

Where the Father's love and glory

Shine in all their brightest rays.

His Almighty power and wisdom

All creation's works proclaim

Heaven and earth alike confess Him

As the ever great I AM.

When we see Him as the Victim

Bound upon Golgotha's cross

For our guilt and folly stricken

Bearing judgment due to us

Lord, we own, with hearts adoring,

He has loved us unto blood;

Glory, glory everlasting

Be unto the Lamb of God!

(J.G. Deck)

# CHAPTER SIX: MY SERVANT (JOHN TERRELL)

One of the very significant titles of the Lord Jesus in the Scriptures, and one that is rich in teaching about His person and work, is 'My Servant'. It is a title given in the Old Testament prophetic scriptures, and Isaiah chapter 42 is our first text about the Lord Jesus as the Servant of Jehovah:

> "Behold! My Servant whom I uphold, My Elect One in whom My soul delights! I have put My Spirit upon Him; He will bring forth justice to the Gentiles. He will not cry out, nor raise His voice, nor cause His voice to be heard in the street. A bruised reed He will not break, and smoking flax He will not quench; He will bring forth justice for truth. He will not fail nor be discouraged, till He has established justice in the earth; and the coastlands shall wait for His law."

What completely assures us that these words belong to the Lord Jesus is their quotation in the twelfth chapter of the gospel according to Matthew. There the Master had come into conflict with the Pharisees who disputed with Him about which acts were legitimate on the Sabbath. In the quiet of the synagogue, the Lord graciously restored the withered hand of a man doubtless condemned to permanent unemployment as a result of his disability - all in all a pretty typical day in the Lord's kindly, unobtrusive ministry of healing and grace. And the Holy Spirit, through Matthew, directly applies the words we have quoted from Isaiah 42. 'My Servant', chosen, Spirit anointed, serving the divine purpose in quiet gentleness and sympathetic care for men and women in desperate need - a lovely presentation of the grace of God in Christ (Matthew 12:15-21).

Now it's very interesting to note that the designation 'Servant', far from being a term of disparagement or condescension in the Old Testament scriptures, is one that is applied to nearly all of the great men of their day. Without quoting all the scripture references, we note that 'Servant' is the description of no less worthies than Abraham, Moses, Joshua, David, Elijah and many others. 'Servant' is a designation also applied to Israel as a nation. Similarly, Paul and the other apostles speak of themselves as servants, bondservants of Jesus Christ. It conjures up images of humility, obedience, faithfulness. And why not, we may ask, concerning the attitudes and actions of men and women in relation to their God? Why not indeed! Men consider it an honour today to serve the monarch or president of their country, whether in high office or in a more lowly role.

But the amazing aspect of the subject is its application to the Lord Jesus Christ 'who, being in the form of God, did not consider it robbery to be equal with God, but made Himself of no reputation, taking the form of a bondservant ... and became obedient to the point of death, even the death of the cross'. There are four servant passages in the prophecy of Isaiah each presenting varying shades of teaching about the One who was to come. They are in chapters 49,50,52 and 53 as well as chapter 42. Through all of them shine God's delight in His holy Servant.

In chapter 49 we have Him depicted as a polished shaft in God's quiver. His mouth is like a sharp sword, and He receives the promise that God will be glorified in Him and, "'I will also give You as a light to the Gentiles, that You should be My salvation to the ends of the earth." Passage after passage from the New Testament about the Lord spring to mind from such words. 'Out of His mouth', said John in Revelation chapter 1, 'went a sharp two-edged sword' and, "Go therefore and make disciples of all the nations..." was the command to His appointed men as they looked symbolically from the mountain in Galilee to the ends of the earth.

In Isaiah chapter 50, there is a sketch of the whole odyssey of salvation from the words "He awakens My ear to hear as the learned" through to the sufferings of such words as, "I gave My back to those who struck Me ... I did not hide My face from shame and spitting"; and the supreme challenge to the adversary, "Who will contend with Me? Let us stand together." But it is in Isaiah chapters 52 and 53 that we have the richest presentation of Jehovah's suffering Servant. Here the Servant, destined to be exalted and very high, is seen with visage 'marred more than any man, and His form more than the sons of men'. Yet kings, we are told would shut their mouths at Him one day when what had not been hitherto told them they would see. 'Every eye will see Him, even they who pierced Him' are the words through John in Revelation 1:7.

Isaiah's clearest Messianic prophecy of all is in chapter 53. We treasure the passage beginning, 'He was wounded for our transgressions ... and the LORD has laid on Him the iniquity of us all'. Then the fearful turbulence dies down as we come to the lovely promise, 'He shall see the labor of His soul and be satisfied. By His knowledge My righteous Servant shall justify many ... Therefore I will divide Him a portion with the great, and He shall divide the spoil with the strong.' Our thoughts carry over again quite unbidden to the profound address of Paul to the Philippians concerning:

> "Christ Jesus, who, being in the form of God, did not consider it robbery to be equal with God, but made Himself of no reputation, taking the form of a bondservant, and coming in the likeness of men. And being found in appearance as a man, He humbled Himself and became obedient to the point of death, even the death of the cross. Therefore God

also has highly exalted Him and given Him the Name which is above every name, that at the Name of Jesus every knee should bow, of those in heaven, and of those on earth, and of those under the earth, and that every tongue should confess that Jesus Christ is Lord, to the glory of God the Father."

What a presentation of the Servant of Jehovah! And, says the apostle, "Let this mind be in you". For although the supreme purpose of the Servanthood of Jesus Christ was the sacrifice and suffering of the cross, His servant life was for an example to His own in their relations with Him and with one another. Consider a basin, water and a towel in an upstairs room in Jerusalem, and the Master washing His disciples' feet. "Do you know what I have done to you?"

Did they? Do we? The same gracious One gently reminded His men, "I am among you as the One who serves" (Luke 22:27). And the disciples learned something of the amazing truth of this matter for, in presenting their Master in gospel preaching, the apostles spoke of the God of our fathers glorifying His Servant Jesus; of God having raised up His Servant Jesus. In prayer they spoke of Pontius Pilate, the Gentiles, and the people of Israel being gathered together against your holy Servant Jesus; and of signs and wonders being done through the Name of your holy Servant Jesus (see Acts 3:13-15; 4:25-30). These men had watched Jesus, their Master, and they never forgot what they saw. There are several words used for servant and service in the New Testament, the most striking and significant means bondservant. That is the word in Philippians chapter 2. May the amazing truth of the self-emptying of the Son of God to take the form of a bondservant, never cease to melt and challenge our hearts.

From the realm of light and glory

Came the Son of God as Man,

To unfold the wondrous story

Veiled in God's eternal plan.

As Jehovah's servant treading

Sin-stained earth with heavenly grace,

Ever onward, never faltering

All His steps we love to trace.

(Tom Hyland)

# CHAPTER SEVEN: THE MESSIAH (JOHN TERRELL)

We come now to consider a title of Jesus which has special relevance for the Jewish people, and around which there revolved much of the religious controversy that prevailed during His years of earthly ministry. That title is 'Messiah' and in this case 'title' is the more accurate word than 'name' for us to use, as we shall see.

Stand with me for a moment in the judgement hall of Caiaphas the High Priest of Israel in what was very likely the year A.D. 33. It is Passover season and an early, though in fact illegitimate, meeting of the Sanhedrin has been convened. Before the High Priest stands a solitary prisoner, composed and quietly dignified. To confusing and confused allegations, He had disdained to answer. Now the High Priest rises solemnly to his feet in response to a statement vindictively and inaccurately attributed to the prisoner.

"Do You answer nothing?" he demands in imperious tones. "What is it these men testify against You? ... I put You under oath by the living God: Tell us if You are the Christ, the Son of God!" The reply is neither delayed nor fudged. "It is as you said." In other words, 'Indeed, I am.' The high priestly garments are then ceremoniously torn, and the outraged declaration is, "He has spoken blasphemy!" The scene we have depicted, as recorded in Matthew 26:62-65 sums up the Jewish concept of their expected Messiah at the time the Anointed One of God appeared among them, unrecognised and unacknowledged. For the term 'the Christ' is the Greek translation of 'Messiah' itself from a word of Hebrew origin meaning 'anointing'. The Messiah is the Anointed One. That very fact immediately associates the bearer of the title with the offices of prophet, priest and king, all of which involved a ceremonial anointing for their religious and royal offices.

The defining moment of history had arrived for the Jewish nation on that Passover occasion in A.D. 33. For centuries, the Jewish people had studied, meditated on, and anticipated the concept of the Messiah. They read about Him in the writings of their most respected prophets. He was to be the agent of the God of Israel for the fulfilment of the destiny of the nation. He was the coming One who would fulfil all the aspirations of the prophets. In His royalty and conquering valour, He would spring in genealogy from the family of David. Caiaphas, the High Priest before whom Jesus stood on that fateful day, was very familiar with Isaiah's resonant words:

> "There shall come forth a Rod from the stem of Jesse, and a Branch shall grow out of his roots. The Spirit of the Lord shall rest upon Him, the Spirit of wisdom and understanding, the Spirit of counsel and might, the Spirit of knowledge and of the fear of the Lord. His delight is in the fear of the Lord, and He shall not judge by the sight of His eyes, nor decide by the hearing of His ears; but with righteousness He shall judge the poor, and decide with equity for the meek of the earth; He shall strike the earth with the rod of His mouth, and with the breath of His lips He shall slay the wicked. Righteousness shall be the belt of His loins, and faithfulness the belt of His waist" (Isaiah 11:1-5).

This was but one of the stirring depictions of the Messiah in the ancient prophets of Israel. Who was this itinerant preacher-rabbi from Nazareth, of all places, to presume upon such a title? But had not the same prophet who wrote of the Messiah that "the government will be upon His shoulder ... of the increase of His government and peace there will be no end", also given God's people a challenging picture of One whose "visage was marred more than any man, and His form more than the sons of men yet who would sprinkle many nations; kings would shut their mouths at Him"?

Also about 'a man of sorrows' upon whom Jehovah would lay 'the iniquity of us all' - for whom the Lord would "divide Him a portion with the great, and ... divide the spoil with the strong?" And all because "He poured out His soul unto death ... was numbered with the transgressors ... bore the sin of many ... made intercession for the transgressors" (Isaiah 9:6,7; 52:14,15; 53:3,6,12)? Oh yes, the words of Isaiah 11 were very welcome, thank you, to the Jewish religious leaders to promote a national ego-trip, but not the sublime story of a suffering Messiah whose real power was in sacrificial love, in vicarious sin-bearing, who was to reign from a cross in the hearts of men and women before returning to the highest seat of heaven.

The actual word 'Messiah' only appears as such twice in the English New Testament while 'Christ' occurs some 35 times in the synoptics; and we have referred several times in this series to Peter's monumental confession, "You are the Christ, the Son of the living God." It is, interestingly enough, in John's gospel that the word 'Messiah' is used. In John 1:41 Andrew declares to Simon his brother, "We have found the Messiah." And then from an outcast woman by a lonely well in Samaria comes the claim, "I know that Messiah is coming," followed by the challenge to her fellow townspeople, "Come, see a Man who told me all things that I ever did. Could this be the Christ?" (John 4:25,29). So the mighty revelation, denied to the crooked and unbelieving Caiaphas, was given to uncomplicated hearts ready to receive the Lord by faith.

Calvary past, and Isaiah's prophecy of suffering fulfilled, the apostles of Jesus Christ went out in Holy Spirit boldness to fulfil His commission of evangelism. Their witness was first to the Jewish nation, and to begin with they vigorously asserted the Messiahship of Jesus their Master.

Two occasions come to mind. From Peter came the words, "Therefore let all the house of Israel know assuredly that God has made this Jesus, whom you crucified, both Lord and Christ" (Acts 2:36). And concerning Paul's early days of witness it was written, "Saul increased all the more in strength, and confounded the Jews who dwelt in Damascus, proving that this Jesus is the Christ" (Acts 9:22).

Of course, the religious Jews always saw in the title 'Messiah' a glorious future of triumph and exalted authority. And they were not entirely wrong in this. The tragedy lay in their blind rejection of a suffering, sin-atoning Christ of Calvary. Truly the day will dawn when Isaiah's powerful words will come to pass, "He shall strike the earth with the rod of His mouth, and with the breath of His lips He shall slay the wicked" (Isaiah 11:4). Then also Micah's prediction will be realised about the One to come forth out of Bethlehem Ephratha who "shall stand and feed His flock in the strength of the LORD, in the majesty of the name of the LORD His God; ... For now He shall be great to the ends of the earth; and this One shall be peace" (Micah 5:4,5).

The title 'Messiah' does have a special resonance for the Jewish nation, but all who love and serve the Anointed One of Jehovah rejoice together in the glories of the prophetic, priestly, and kingly offices of Him who wore the crown of thorns at Calvary for us men and for our salvation; and whom God has highly exalted and given the Name that is above every name.

# CHAPTER EIGHT: THE PROPHET (JOHN TERRELL)

In the next three chapters of this book we shall look together at three titles as applied to the Jesus, namely Prophet, Priest, and King; and the aspects of His divine ministry which are connected with them. So in considering firstly the title and office of prophet, let us eavesdrop for a moment on one of the most remarkable encounters described in the gospel narrative. It was late afternoon and the journey must be on foot - all seven and a half miles from Jerusalem to their home village. Two weary, utterly bewildered disciples talking together of all these "things which (had) happened". "What things?" asked their newly found fellow traveller. "The things concerning Jesus of Nazareth, who was a Prophet mighty in deed and word before God and all the people".

Most readers will recognise the story and feel again that spine-tingling excitement that the Emmaus road always evokes in the believer rejoicing in the risen Saviour. The Master soon began to lift the thoughts and spirits of the disciples as He launched into what must have been one of the most enlightening discourses human ears have ever heard. For, beginning at Moses and all the Prophets, He expounded to them in all the Scriptures the things concerning Himself. Now what is of particular interest to us right now is the way in which the Emmaus road disciples spoke of their crucified Lord – "a Prophet mighty in deed and word". And then, the Master's choice of themes for His self-revealing discourse to them - beginning at (Revised Version: "from") Moses and all the Prophets.

Clearly, those who heard and companied with Jesus during His ministry had come to think of Him as an outstanding prophet who established His credentials by being mighty in deed and word. This expression evokes in our minds, doesn't it, the leadership and instruction of a Moses; or the miracles and ministry of an Elijah. For to the Israelite, the office and ministry of the prophets were revered and treated with a very wholesome respect. We know how highly God valued His prophets. In Psalm 105 we read that God's command to the nations was, "Do not touch My anointed ones, and do My prophets no harm". And now, as the Lord set about opening up the minds of the two travelling disciples He began with Moses and all the prophets. This was language they would understand and relate to. These two disciples probably knew about the Lord's miracle of raising the dead at Nain. On that occasion the exclamation of the on-lookers was, "A great prophet has risen up among us" and "God has visited His people".

The appearance of a divinely anointed prophet in Israel had always been hailed by the spiritually minded Jew as a real visitation from God. Little wonder the Lord Jesus, the Prophet mighty in deed and word, wept over Jerusalem as He entered the city for the last time before Calvary, and deplored the tragedy, "you did not know the time of your visitation". And all this was in spite of the fact that, when He entered the city initially, the crowd said, "This is Jesus, the Prophet from Nazareth of Galilee". The disciples had earlier told the Lord that many of the people had identified Him as Elijah or Jeremiah, or one of the prophets returned to life.

So let us go back a bit and consider for a moment how the title and office of prophet had emerged in Israel; most importantly how God saw it, and the vital part it played in His self-revelation to His people. In Deuteronomy chapter 18, Moses is in full flow as he recounts to the nation the history of God's dealing with them. In verses 15-22 of that chapter, He reminds them of a promise God had made to him, and repeats the words for emphasis in His address to them. "The Lord your God will raise up for you a Prophet like me from your midst, from your brethren" and, quoting God's own words, he declared, "I ... will put My words in His mouth, and He shall speak to them all that I command Him. And it shall be that whoever will not hear My words, which He speaks in My Name, I will require it of him".

Some versions of the Bible print the word 'prophet' in this passage with a capital 'P' indicating the translator's conviction that this is a prophecy of the coming Christ. Indeed, students of the Word, seeking Christ in all the Scriptures, can hardly have much doubt about the import of this promise. It is certain from the gospels' narrative that the Lord acknowledged the title Prophet as applicable to Himself. We remember His words when His own folk in Nazareth rejected Him. "A prophet is not without honor except in his own country and in his own house" (Matthew 13:57). Then, speaking of His impending sacrifice and death, He said, "It cannot be that a prophet should perish outside of Jerusalem" (Luke 13:33). Here was the promised prophet of Deuteronomy 18 with the words of God in His mouth, commanding the acceptance and accountability of all who heard. God would require it of them, as Moses had declared.

So it always was, in varying degrees, for all the prophets of Israel. They were men controlled and inspired by God; men who not only often foretold the future, but even more importantly, were the authoritative bearers of the words of God to His people. The word most commonly used in the Old Testament for 'prophet' carried the thought of bubbling over; of Spirit-filling which could not be contained, but had to have release in the fearless and faithful speaking out of the Word of the Lord. The prophet was a man sent from God, sometimes primarily to His people, as in Judges chapter 6 where we read that the Lord sent a prophet to the children of Israel; sometimes to an individual, as with the unnamed man of God who was sent to Eli with a powerful message which has lived on in its solemn promise and warning, "those who honor Me I will honor, and those who despise Me shall be lightly esteemed" (1 Samuel 2:30). In Jeremiah's case the prophetic commission was global in its scope: "I ordained you a prophet to the nations".

The prophetic ministry of Christ embraced all three dimensions - the individual, the people-wide and the universal. In Ephesians chapter 1:9-10 (in the Revised Version) we read that it was God's good pleasure 'to sum up all things' in Christ. This is certainly true of the way in which the Lord Jesus brought to wonderful consummation the prophetic ministry of the great men of God of Israel's history. We read that the law and the prophets were until John. To John the Baptist it was given to introduce to Israel the great Prophet of our God of whom Moses had spoken.

If the prophet's chief function was to give forth the Word of God with faithfulness and authority, none fulfilled this like the Son of God. God, 'who at various times and in various ways spoke in time past to the fathers by the prophets, has in these last days spoken to us by His Son' (Hebrews 1:1-2). The words of the old hymn say it all:

Great Prophet of our God,

Our tongue would bless Thy Name;

By Thee the joyful news

Of our salvation came;

The joyful news of sins forgiven,

Of hell subdued,

Of peace with heaven.

(Isaac Watts)

# CHAPTER NINE: THE GREAT HIGH PRIEST (JOHN TERRELL)

We now come to the subject of the priesthood of the Lord Jesus. Immediately there come to mind the commanding words of Psalm 110, "You are a priest forever". And there is perhaps no psalm in the entire Psalter which more clearly and explicitly speaks of the coming priestly One who is called 'my Lord' by David. Clearly it was central to God's eternal purpose for His Son that He should be a priest; and, as we shall see, a priest in very special and unique circumstances. The Old Testament scriptures furnish us with rich illustrations and types of Christ's priesthood.

The choice of the tribe of Levi as the priestly tribe of Israel was one with very far-reaching significance and consequences. They had to stand between men and God and, in the case of the High Priest, to enter the very presence of God on behalf of the people to carry out vital services there as their representative. These services were central to the continuing covenant relationship between God and His people. Not only were there precise instructions to Moses about their anointing with oil and marking with the blood of sacrifice, but the very clothing they wore must be in accord with the divine prescription.

All of these things, linked to the multifarious tasks and functions of the priests, underlined the solemn importance God attached to their role as standing between Him, in all His untarnished holiness, and His people. This is, of course, most strongly evident in the case of the High Priest of Israel who, on the annual Day of Atonement entered the immediate presence of God in the inner sanctuary of the tabernacle or temple. So the Old Testament priestly role-model for our Lord Jesus Christ is the High Priest, and little wonder that He receives the extended title of 'Great High Priest' (Hebrews 4:14). In John 17:19, in the course of what is often referred to as the Lord's high priestly prayer for His disciples, anticipating His future heavenly office of High Priest, we have the remarkable words, "For their sakes I sanctify Myself, that they also may be sanctified by the truth."

This marvel, the self-dedication and consecration of the Son of God for a perfect example to His own, and for His priestly service for them in heaven, finds its fuller exposition in the epistle to the Hebrews. This is the New Testament book uniquely dealing with the sanctuary service of the people of God, and the High Priestly service of Christ on their behalf. Psalm 110 is a song of praise and promise to the triumphant Victor of Calvary. It opens with the command, "Sit at My right hand, till I make Your enemies Your footstool." It speaks of 'the rod of His strength'; of 'the day of His power'; of 'the beauties of holiness'; and climaxes with, "The LORD has sworn and will not relent, 'You are a priest forever according to the order of Melchizedek.'"

Now these last words open a remarkable vista of the unique high priestly ministry of Christ in heaven for, while much of the nature and content of the Lord's priestly function in heaven today derives from the priesthood of Aaron, its rank, or order, was very different. The secret of this lies in the words, 'according to the order of Melchizedek' and, as already stated, the textbook of this subject is the epistle to the Hebrews. In Hebrews chapter 2 we read of the Lord Jesus that "in all things He had to be made like His brethren, that He might be a merciful and faithful High Priest in things pertaining to God". This was the remarkable starting point of His qualifications for priestly office. The Lord Jesus was 'called of God' as we have seen from Psalm 110, which Psalm also confirms that He was made a priest by the oath of God.

References to these points will be found in Hebrews chapters 5 and 7. Then we have His experience of temptation, offering up prayers in the days of His flesh, learning the cost of obedience through suffering, through which He was 'perfected', or made complete, in His preparatory experience for priesthood. He offered Himself a sacrifice and, in Hebrews chapter 4 we read, 'passed through the heavens.' Let us pause and ask ourselves, "Who is this Person who has so totally and irrevocably dedicated Himself to the heavenly service of His people? Was not the suffering of the cross, to bring us eternal forgiveness and salvation more than enough to expect from the holy, spotless Son of God from heaven; enough to complete the work of Calvary; to revert to His rightful place above where He is so much better than the angels; and to await the day of the final redemption of His purchased possession, the Church, His Body, having sent the Comforter, the Spirit of truth, to be with His own?" No! Not so. He was also preparing Himself, consecrating Himself, for a rich and amazingly gracious ministry in heaven for a people on earth whom He has purchased with His own blood.

What is that ministry, that devoted service in which He is unfailing in heaven? From Hebrews 2 we learn that He "succours", or helps, when we are tempted; He invites us to come near to the throne of grace to obtain mercy and find grace. He actually appears before God making intercession for us. He ensures that we have access to all the benefits and blessings of the new covenant, and He presents our sacrifices of praise to God. In all of this He far excels the scope of the priestly services of Aaron and his sons for the people of Israel in the past, though in basic nature His work is similar.

But, as we have already noted, there is something else very special indeed about the priesthood of Christ. We remember the promise of Psalm 110, "You are a priest forever according to the order of Melchizedek". Herein lies the secret of the surpassing excellence of the priestly work of our Lord compared to all the priests of Israel's history. Not just a total contrast of quality compared with the shameful desecration of the priestly office by men like Annas and Caiaphas who dared to sit in judgement on God's Anointed. Something far greater.

For in the Melchizedek role model, three glorious principles were enshrined waiting to be fulfilled in our Great High Priest. First, His priesthood was superior to Aaron's to the point of perfection (Hebrews 7:26-28). Secondly, it was eternal. Thirdly, it joined together two offices, something hitherto strictly forbidden in Israel, though portrayed in Melchizedek, the offices of King and Priest. For God's Christ alone was the conjunction of these two roles reserved. His priesthood was more excellent than Aaron's; indeed perfect as we have seen. All of this because He was, in contrast to Aaron, sinless and lives in the power of an endless life. Like Melchizedek, He is God's King Priest and that forever.

The main references to many of these points are in Hebrews chapter 7. So much more could be said about our merciful and faithful High Priest, beautifully described in Hebrews 7:26 as holy, harmless, undefiled, separate from sinners; about His sanctuary service for a sanctified, subject people today who strive to give expression to the truths of God's house with its high and holy privileges of worship in the holy place above. This we read of in Hebrews 10:19-25, "Therefore, brethren, having boldness to enter the Holiest ... by a new and living way which He consecrated for us, through the veil, that is, His flesh, and having a High Priest over the house of God let us draw near ..."

It is a contemplation that is rich in spiritual values, instructive about the glorious Person of the risen Lord; and draws the spirit very close to the deeply caring love and concern that our beloved Lord has for His own. It whets our appetite for heaven where He is engaged in this amazingly gracious service; and, until that day, adds reassurance about our access to God through Him, both to get and to give: to get help, mercy and grace; to give worship and our sacrifice of praise.

In Christ the Lord our eyes behold

A thousand glories more

Than the rich gems and polished gold

The sons of Aaron wore.

They first their own sin-offering brought

To purge themselves from sin;

His life was pure, without a spot,

And all his nature clean.

Their range was earth, nor higher soared,

The heaven of heavens is His;

There in His majesty, the Lord

A Priest for ever is.

Eternal glories crown His name,

As Prophet, Priest and King;

Soon heaven and earth shall sound his fame,

Each day fresh praises bring.

(Isaac Watts)

# CHAPTER TEN: KING (OF KINGS) (JOHN TERRELL

---

Now we come to the last of the titles associated with anointing. That is, KING. First of all, let us stand together where every disciple of the Lord Jesus Christ has stood many times in spirit - a subdued spirit - by a Roman crucifixion just outside the walls of Jerusalem; a scene so full of squalor and brutality that the human mind recoils from it in horror. Three crosses; three victims. But over one in the centre is a notice, variously called a superscription or an accusation, 'THIS IS JESUS, THE KING OF THE JEWS'. Here surely is the throne from which the Saviour will always reign supreme in the hearts of His own.

Here the King of all the ages

Throned in light ere worlds could be

Robed in mortal flesh is dying,

Crucified by sin for me.

(F.W. Faber)

As the crowd chanted, "Crucify!" the Roman governor demanded of them, "Shall I crucify your King?" And back came an answer more fateful for Israel perhaps than for any other, "We have no king but Caesar!" (John 19:15). Will the loving response of our hearts not be:

King of my life, I crown Thee now,

Thine shall the glory be;

Lest I forget Thy thorn-crowned brow,

Lead me to Calvary.

Lest I forget Gethsemane,

Lest I forget Thine agony,

Lest I forget Thy love to me,

Lead me to Calvary.

(J.E. Mussey)

Few contemplations of the Person of Christ evoke more adoration and worship than His royalty. Throughout Holy Scripture, God is presented to men as King. David said in Psalm 29:10, "The LORD sits as King forever". And we remember how Micah the prophet wrote, "But you, Bethlehem Ephrathah, though you are little among the thousands of Judah, yet out of you shall come forth to Me the One to be Ruler in Israel, whose goings forth are from of old, from everlasting."

So in the process of God's perfect time, the memorable question was asked by the sages from the Orient, "Where is He who has been born King of the Jews? For we have seen His star in the East and have come to worship Him" (Matthew 2:2). There was none of the pomp of royalty in evidence either in Bethlehem or in the Nazareth years. Indeed, throughout the three-year ministry of the Lord, His kingship was in the background of His kingdom teaching which was initially and primarily to Israel. Only as Jesus approached the end of His ministry and Calvary loomed in view, did His kingship again come into prominence. It is true that the people once tried to take Him to make Him king. But they had no clear perception of the matter and the Lord knew it well.

So the onward march of the redemptive purpose of God continued and the moment of fulfilment arrived for the ancient prophecy of Zechariah. As the disciples go off to Bethphage to find the donkey, we are reminded by Matthew of this wonderful prophecy. "Tell the daughter of Zion, 'Behold, your King is coming to you, lowly, and sitting on a donkey, a colt, the foal of a donkey'" (Matthew 21:5). Some perceptive glimpse of the fulfilment of prophecy seems to be revealed in the words of the multitude of the disciples who cried out, "Blessed is the King who comes in the name of the Lord! Peace in heaven and glory in the highest" (Luke 19:38).

As Pilate proceeded to examine the Saviour he could not escape the question, "Are You a king then?" Jesus answered without hesitation, "You say rightly that I am a king. For this cause I was born, and for this cause I have come into the world, that I should bear witness to the truth." He was yet to be described in Scripture as conquering and to conquer, but for now it was very different.

Hath He diadem, as Monarch,

That His brow adorns?

"Yea, a crown, in very surety,

But of thorns."

(J.M. Neale)

And so to Calvary. But now we turn to the inspired chant of the Sons of Korah:

> "My heart is overflowing with a good theme; I recite my composition concerning the King; my tongue is the pen of a ready writer. You are fairer than the sons of men; grace is poured upon Your lips; therefore God has blessed You forever. Gird Your sword upon Your thigh, O Mighty One, with Your glory and Your majesty. And in Your majesty ride prosperously because of truth, humility, and righteousness; and

Your right hand shall teach You awesome things. Your arrows are sharp in the heart of the King's enemies; the peoples fall under You. Your throne, O God, is forever and ever; a scepter of righteousness is the scepter of Your kingdom. You love righteousness and hate wickedness; therefore God, Your God, has anointed You with the oil of gladness more than Your companions" (Psalm 45:1-7).

We can sense the note of excitement that rang in the voices of the sons of Korah as they intoned such words; likewise the exalted spirit of the apostle John as the Holy Spirit led him to write the words:

"I saw heaven opened, and behold, a white horse. And He who sat on him was called Faithful and True, and in righteousness He judges and makes war. His eyes were like a flame of fire, and on His head were many crowns ... And He has on His robe and on His thigh a name written: KING OF KINGS AND LORD OF LORDS'" (Revelation 19:11-16).

Centuries before, the psalmist had conveyed the voice of God in the face of human pride and rebellion. "Yet I have set My King on My holy hill of Zion." And again from the sublime poetry of the Psalms, we have the exultant cry of the host of heaven, "Lift up your heads, O you gates! And be lifted up, you everlasting doors! And the King of glory shall come in. Who is this King of glory?...The LORD of hosts, He is the King of glory" (Psalm 24:7-10).

Let us finally reflect on one remarkable fact about the kingship of Christ. In writing previously about His priesthood, we referred to Melchizedek who, we recall, was priest of God Most High and also King of Salem, King of Peace. No king of Israel was ever allowed to combine the offices of priest and king. Defiance of this law was the downfall of Uzziah, whom Isaiah mourned as a young man when he received his breath-taking vision of 'the King' (Isaiah 6). Only the coming One, the Lord from heaven, was to unite these two great offices of priest and king. "'A priest forever according to the order of Melchizedek" and, "My King on My holy hill of Zion". The Messiah; the Christ; the Anointed of God.

Prophet, Priest and King, behold Him,

Saviour, Shepherd, Christ and Lord;

Heaven's myriads bow before Him,

Praise His Name with one accord.

Saints on earth their voices raising

Shout the praises, bless the Name

Of the One who died to save us,

Jesus evermore the same.

(G.T. Reeve)

# CHAPTER ELEVEN: ALPHA & OMEGA (CRAIG JONES)

Amongst the most wonderful of the names and titles of the Lord Jesus is the trio of titles which the Lord Jesus ascribes to Himself in Revelation 22:13: "I am the Alpha and the Omega, the Beginning and the End, the First and the Last."

The initial impression of these titles is that they effectively say the same thing concerning the Lord's eternal nature and character, helping us to try to grasp what would seem incomprehensible to our finite minds - that the Lord Jesus Christ is, He always has been and always will be. It's also interesting to note that in Revelation 1:8 and 21:6, it is the Lord God who ascribes to Himself the title 'Alpha and Omega'. So, this clearly emphasises not only the Lord Jesus' eternal nature, but also His eternal deity, as He shares the same title that the Lord God uses for Himself, demonstrating their eternal co-existence and unity. Although seeming to express the same truth, this trio of titles reveals subtle differences of emphasis.

**Alpha and Omega**

Alpha and Omega are, of course, the first and last letters of the Greek alphabet, in which the New Testament was written. The purpose of letters is to create words through which communication is made easier and less susceptible to misunderstanding. So in this title, we are considering the Lord Jesus as the Word - the means by which God communicates with us. John 1:1 declares that the Word was with God in the beginning and in verse 14 of that chapter, the one who is referred to as the Word is clearly revealed as the Lord Jesus, who "became flesh and dwelt among us". Revelation 19:11-13 describes the rider on the white horse, who is called Faithful and True, of whom John also states "His name is called The Word of God".

Jesus Christ, the Son of God, is the perfect revelation of the essence and character of God, the most perfect expression of everything that God wants to say to us concerning Himself and His purposes. Jesus Christ is the first and last word in everything to do with His God and Father. The writer to the Hebrews wonderfully encapsulates this truth: "God ... has ... spoken to us by His Son, whom He has appointed heir of all things, through whom also He made the worlds: who being the brightness of His glory and the express image of His person, and upholding all things by the word of His power ..." (Hebrews 1:1-3).

Jesus Himself declared that "the word which you hear is not Mine but the Father's who sent me" (John 14:24). We are reminded too of the poignant parable He spoke to the people, regarding the tenants of the vineyard, to whom the vineyard owner sent his servants that he may receive the fruit of the vineyard. The servants were treated harshly: rejected, beaten and even killed, until finally the vineyard owner said, "I will send my beloved son. Probably they will respect him when they see him" (Luke 20:13). It seems incredible to us that those to whom the Lord Jesus was sent, as a token of love, as the perfect embodiment of the heart of the Father, should so cruelly reject Him, fulfilling Isaiah's prophecy concerning the One who would be "despised and rejected by men, a Man of sorrows and acquainted with grief" (Isaiah 53:3). But He is the One through whom the Sovereign Lord God had chosen to reveal Himself, and His word to all is, "This is My Beloved Son. Hear Him!" (Luke 9:35).

## The Beginning and the End

This is clearly a matter of time, or rather, eternity. The Greek word 'arche' (beginning) essentially means the origin or active cause of something (see W.E. Vine Expository Dictionary of New Testament

Words). Our minds are immediately taken back to John 1:1,2 and we might also consider 1 John 1:1 and Colossians 1:16-18. Through these familiar scriptures, the Holy Spirit categorically teaches us that the Lord Jesus – the eternal Word of God who indeed became human, touchable, of whom many in His day could testify by the proof of their sense-perception - was pre-existent to the creation of the world. When the world had its beginning, the Word already was. The world in fact owes its very existence to the awesome, majestic, creatorial power of the One who is the Word of God. God said in Genesis 1:26, "Let Us make...", a statement that flows on naturally from His other spoken words of creation, clearly implying the on-going joint agency of the Godhead in the creative process. John makes it crystal clear for us – "without Him nothing was made that was made" (John 1:3). Paul further underlines the truth in Colossians 1:16: "For by Him all things were created ... all things were created through Him and for Him". Just as the Lord Jesus is the active cause and origin of the creation, He will also be the One through whom these things will come to an end. 1 Peter 4:7 speaks of "the end of all things" - the same 'all things' that hold together and consist in the Lord Jesus Himself. The time will come when this physical creation will come to an end and the beginning of the end will be ushered in when the Lord Jesus comes back to the air to take those who are His.

**The First and the Last**

The context of this expression, as we have seen, has to do with Christ's unchangeable eternal character: He who is First and Last, the centre and circumference, the co-equal, co-eternal and con-substantial with the Father. The Lord Jesus, in His eternal, divine nature, occupies the place of supreme pre-eminence, honour and exaltation. He is without doubt the First and Foremost in all things.

# SPARKLING FACETS: BIBLE NAMES AND TITLES OF JESUS

We don't need to think too hard to understand why the Lord Jesus so thoroughly deserves such absolute pre-eminence. We need only to go to Colossians 1:15-20 for a reminder of why: "image of the invisible God ... firstborn over all creation ... by Him all things were created ... He is before all things ... in Him all things consist ... He is the head of the body, the church ... the beginning ... firstborn from the dead ... in Him all the fullness should dwell ... by Him to reconcile all things to Himself ... made peace through the blood of His cross".

This is the incomparable Christ, who fully deserves the highest honours, the richest praise and all the glory we can ascribe to Him - He is worthy! Nevertheless we come to realize with deepest humility and amazement that although He is pre-eminent He had to know first and last in a very different aspect too. Like no-one else ever could, Jesus lived out and experienced the reality of His own teaching, "the last will be first and the first will be last". In majestic grace and humility, in inexpressible love, He stepped down from the glorious riches of His place of sovereign splendour, counting it not a prize He "made Himself of no reputation, taking the form of a bondservant ... and being found in appearance as a man, He humbled Himself and became obedient to the point of death, even the death of the cross" (Philippians 2:7-8). He took the lowest place, He became last in the eyes of the world - the eternal, sovereign Word of God, the pre-existent Author of all things, became as "a worm, and no man; a reproach of men, and despised of the people" (Psalm 22:6). Hallelujah, what a Saviour!

> "Therefore God also has highly exalted Him and given Him the name which is above every name, that at the name of Jesus every knee should bow ... and that every tongue should confess that Jesus Christ is Lord, to the glory of God the Father" (Philippians 2:9-11).

Our Saviour knows all about beginnings and endings, and so we can be confident that He will be with us in all our beginnings and endings. Our life's experience is made up of such - some bring anxiety or fear, some bring sorrow, some bring joy and renewed hope. How thankful we are that the Alpha and the Omega, the Beginning and the End, the First and the Last has promised to be with us every step of the way.

# CHAPTER TWELVE: THE ONLY BEGOTTEN (REG PARKER)

---

It's a rewarding meditation to take the time to consider the five references in the New Testament which contain the title, "the Only Begotten Son". David the Psalmist is used by the Spirit of God in the second Psalm to write of the decree as the words of the Son: "I will tell of the decree: The LORD has said to Me, You are My Son; today I have begotten You" (Psalm 2:7).

The day of "begetting" in this verse has been described as the day of eternity, having neither beginning nor end, which has no yesterday or tomorrow. It is a declaration of the eternal counsels of Deity concerning the eternal Son of the eternal Father. In the light of such amazing revelation we can only bow in faith and accept what the Spirit of God has declared. With these thoughts in mind, let us now consider the five occurrences of the title 'the Only Begotten'.

**(1) "We beheld His glory, the glory as of the only begotten from the Father, full of grace and truth" (John 1:14)**

The Greek word for glory is doxa, which really means a notion or an opinion which one has of a thing or a person; so that glory is an expression of esteem, honour, praise and adoration because of the qualities, virtues and attributes seen in any one who deserves praise and celebration. His glory was seen on earth among men. It was a transcending degree of excellence, honour, splendour, praise and worthiness which flowed out of the character of the only begotten of the Father. He was no ordinary person dwelling among men. He was the only Man having a divine nature. All His actions and words were full of grace and truth. He counted others better than Himself and it was impossible for Him to lie (cf. John 8:45). His behaviour showed He was a unique Person. From His conversation it was clear He has a Father. By His actions and ways it was evident He always pleased Him.

He has infinite ability. He can turn water into wine. He can heal people at the point of death without being present with them. He can cure longstanding illness, even from birth. He can take five barley loaves and two fish and feed more than five thousand people. He can walk on the sea. He can open blind eyes, even of someone born blind. These signs were aids to help people believe who He is. The signs showed out or manifested His glory and His disciples believed on Him (John 2:11). But the reaction of the multitude was amazement and fear, and glorifying God they said, 'We have seen strange things today' (Luke 5:26) and 'A great Prophet has risen up among us: and God has visited His people' (Luke 7:16). The glory was not characteristic of man's sin-tainted ability, but characteristic of a sinless, Supreme Being (John 9:30). The excellence, honour, esteem and praise-worthiness was glory as of the only begotten from the Father. The character of the Father was seen in the glory of the Son who came into the world to save sinners.

**(2) "The only begotten Son, who is in the bosom of the Father; He has declared Him" (John 1:18)**

It has often been pointed out that the term 'only begotten' does not necessarily mean an only child but rather one upon whom affection is concentrated (see Genesis 22:2,12,16; Hebrews 11:17). Never at any time has man seen God. Any knowledge we have of God can only come through the Son of God and the Word of God by the operation of the Spirit of God in our hearts. One of the great mysteries of the Godhead is the eternal relationships between God the Father, God the Son and God the Holy Spirit. Since the relationships are eternal they can never be severed. If severance were possible, then when the Word became flesh He would no longer have been in the bosom of the Father. In fact although He became flesh He is at the same time in the bosom of the Father.

This scripture establishes and declares that the eternal Son, being the centre of the affection of the Father, dwells in the bosom of the Father from all eternity to all eternity. Who then is more fitted and able to declare to men all that the Father is? Who also is more able to be used by the Spirit of God to convey this fact to men, than the follower of the Lord Jesus, who is described five times as the disciple whom Jesus loved, and frequently reclined in His bosom (see John 13:23 etc.)?

**(3) "... God so loved the world that He gave His only begotten Son, that whoever believes in Him should not perish but have everlasting life" (John 3:16)**

Some of the most profound statements regarding the Godhead are found in John's Gospel and his epistles. John by the Spirit reveals the very nature or essence of God in three declarations: God is Spirit, God is Light and God is Love. They essentially describe God's substance (Greek: hupostasis) out of which flow God's image or likeness (Greek: charakter). By way of illustration, the word 'hupostasis' may be represented by the form of a seal, which when applied to wax, the precise and accurate likeness of the seal (hupostasis) is impressed in the wax (charakter). Similarly, a coin which is struck from a die bears the precise and accurate likeness of the die. So it is that the character or image of God springs from God's nature or essence.

The love of God has been demonstrated to the world by the Father giving the Son so that the world might live through Him. God's love has two facets contained in two Greek words – "agape" and "philia". The first is not the love of affection drawn out by the excellency or desirability of its objects. It has been described as loving that has no cause outside itself. The other is distinguished from the first in that it represents tender affection. Both words are used for the love of the Father for the Son (John 3:35; 5:20).

In John 3:16 the intensity and profundity of God's love for the world is stated. God so loved that He gave. The love of men tires, wanes and varies. Our love is ofttimes low, but the love of God is eternal, unchanging and enduring as His nature. When God's creature man fell short of His glory by Adam's transgression, God intervened in human affairs to save man on the basis of agape love. He loved the world even though the world was lost and ruined by the Fall. The intensity of agape love for the world is measured by the statement, "God so loved ... that He gave His only begotten Son".

The degree of giving enabled God to extend to everyone who accepts the gift of His only begotten Son freedom from sin's penalty. To perish does not mean annihilation, but rather to suffer ruin and loss, not of existence or being, but of well-being. In love, God gave to save from ruin and loss. In believing, man receives the gift of eternal well-being and eternal happiness.

**(4) "He who believes in Him is not condemned; but he who does not believe is condemned already, because he has not believed in the name of the only begotten Son of God" (John 3:18)**

In His Word, the Bible, God has revealed that all the actions and words of men are subject to His judgements. All men from Adam onwards are accountable to the eternal, Triune God. Sinning is falling short of God's requirements. Sin, both root and branch, was judicially dealt with on the cross by the Lord Jesus, the only begotten Son, to His Father's entire satisfaction. By the grace and mercy of God extended to men an individual may know annulment of sin by simple trust in what God has said in His Word and what God has done through His Son at Calvary.

The person who does not trust or does not believe on the Name of God's only begotten Son is considered by God to be judged already for his or her sin and sins. Believing the salvation associated with His Name wipes out our sin and sins. It wipes the slate clean. Unbelief treats the giving of God's Son with contempt, and for such treatment there can only be the judgement of God on the person who so behaves. The Scriptures are perfectly clear, the judgement rests upon them or as another passage in John says, the wrath of God abides or remains upon him.

The Father loves the Son with a love that has no cause outside itself and has given into His hands eternal life to give to those who believe on His Name. He therefore that has the Son has the life, and believing on His Name is the key to God removing judgement and man obtaining eternal life.

**(5) "In this the love of God was manifested toward us, that God has sent His only begotten Son into the world, that we might live through Him" (1 John 4:9)**

This verse is the complement of John 3:16. In that case, God so loved that He gave His only begotten Son. It is whoever you are. Here it is more personal. In our case, God's love is brought to the light by the sending of His only begotten Son into the world.

In summary: John 3:16 states the motive, which is primary, having results in the future. 1 John 4:9 states the action flowing out of the motive. John 3:16 states the purpose or aim of God's love for the future. 1 John 4:9 states the result of rejecting the Son of God's love. Through His Son comes not only life to men from God but also the possibility of living that eternal life on earth here and now.

"We laud the everlasting Word,

The Father's only Son,

God manifestly seen and heard,

And heaven's beloved One,

Worthy the name of Jesus now

That every knee therein should bow.

In Him most perfectly expressed,

The Father's glories shine;

Of the full Deity possessed,

Eternally divine.

Worthy the name of Jesus now

That every knee therein should bow.

True image of the infinite

Whose essence is concealed,

Brightness of uncreated light

The heart of God revealed.

Worthy the name of Jesus now

That every knee therein should bow.

(J. Conder)

# CHAPTER THIRTEEN: THE FAITHFUL WITNESS (D.W. MILLAR)

The Lord Jesus Christ is God's great and faithful witness. The book of the Revelation of Jesus Christ opens by setting before us this divinely-given title, "... Jesus Christ ... the faithful witness" (read Revelation 1:4-7). He has spoken to men and though at present He is hidden from their eyes, the earth is full of His testimony and this scripture reveals that the time will come when every eye shall see Him.

In the vast work of creation, Christ the Son of God witnessed many of the divine attributes by the work of His fingers. "For since the creation of the world His invisible attributes are clearly seen, being understood by the things that are made, even His eternal power and Godhead" (Romans 1:20). When we observe with enlightened eyes the manifold diversity of nature's marvels, we discern handiwork of God's faithful Witness.

But when He was on earth mingling with men and women, the favoured human race had a unique opportunity of looking upon Him and listening to His faithful testimony. Many men and women had borne witness before, but at last God was speaking in the very Person of His Son. He said of Himself and His testimony: "My witness is true, for I know where I came from and where I am going" (John 8:14). Men said of Him: "No man ever spoke like this man" (John 7:46). God said: "This is My beloved Son. Hear Him" (Luke 9:35).

In resurrection power and glory, as unfolded in the book of the Revelation of Jesus Christ, he is twice described as the Faithful Witness. Men ignore what He has to say at their peril. In Revelation 1:10-20, we are given a detailed description of His appearance in His glory as the risen Son of God, at the sight of whom John fell down as one dead. His all-seeing eyes observe all that is going on in these churches and He gives praise, or blame, as One who knows all the circumstances. Again and again He says, "I know": "I know your works", "I know ... where you dwell", "I know your ... tribulation" etc. Indeed, it is because of His complete and perfect knowledge that He is God's faithful witness. Other witnesses have made, and will make, mistakes but He is always faithful and true. What He has to say to the churches is written in one book which is sent to all of them. The faults found in these churches may occur in greater or lesser degree in any assembly.

At the beginning of the letter to Laodicea (Revelation 3:14-22), this title of Christ is mentioned a second time, emphasizing in the solemn words that follow, the testimony of One who, because He is the Faithful Witness, overlooks nothing that requires His judgement, just as He misses nothing which calls for His commendation.

Sadly, although He says "I know your works", He found nothing in them for His praise! His letter to Laodicea is a just, unbiased appraisal of the exact condition there, and what a shock it must have given them! We have here a picture of complacency and self-deception, the worst condition any church or disciple can get into a condition where Satan can find a most promising field for his activity. If there can be found reason for satisfaction in any church it is to be traced only to the richness of Christ. "No flesh should glory before God", but rather "glory in Christ Jesus". Any feelings of self-satisfaction are directly traceable to the devil, who is the great deceiver and specializes in self-deception.

"I counsel you" (verse 18). His words to other churches are commands, but He appeals to Laodicea, as if to say, "Wake up and listen to My advice". "Buy from Me gold", He says. Gold speaks of divine glory, and this stands out in contrast to the condition of this church - wretched, poor, blind, naked. They had become the very opposite of God's purpose for a church of God. God's purpose is that we should become "partakers of the divine nature" (2 Peter 1:4). While God gives us gifts of inestimable value, yet there are other costly things which must be bought. Salvation, for example, is a free gift which cannot be bought by us, but some things the disciple can gain only by giving to God, or perhaps giving up for God. "Buy the truth, and do not sell it", said Solomon.

No disciple can ever lay hold on divine truth and make it a valued possession without paying the price for it. But God gives a hundredfold in return for our small sacrifices. Christ spreads before us His incomparable riches. He also refers to white garments which are associated with righteous acts, and eyesalve so that eyes may be opened to discern the true riches. To the latter the Holy Spirit testifies through Paul having: "the eyes of your understanding being enlightened; that you may know what is the hope of His calling, what are the riches of the glory of His inheritance in the saints" (Ephesians 1:18).

The severe words of reproof are a sign of His love; chastening is proof of His love. He, out of whose mouth proceeds a sharp two-edged sword, desires that we should become living and active like the word on which the church should feed. Not only can material riches close the eyes to the things of God, but also close the ear to the voice of Christ who stands at the door. How solemn are the words to the church at Laodicea, "If anyone hear My voice". This is the ultimate appeal of a grieving Lord. There should be no question of "If". He said, "My sheep hear My voice". He should occupy the central place in the assembly, every ear listening for His voice. Even as the judgement of this church is the most solemn of all, so the promised reward to the overcomer is the greatest of all: "I will grant to sit with Me on My throne, as I also overcame and sat down with My Father on His throne".

Many Old Testament scriptures portray the character and foreshadow the work of the Lord Jesus Christ in the present day and dispensation. In Proverbs 8 the wisdom of Christ from everlasting to everlasting is set forth, the wisdom of His Person and the wisdom of His works, the rich substance of His recompense "Better than gold, yes, than fine gold" (verse 19). Verses 20 and 21 seem to foreshadow the Revelation manifestation of the risen Son of God walking in the midst of the churches: "I traverse the way of righteousness, in the midst of the paths of justice, that I may cause those who love me to inherit wealth, that I may fill their treasuries."

His ways are righteous, His acts are just, and His rewards a rich inheritance. His great purpose and desire for His people are expressed in the words of Paul's prayer for the Ephesian saints: "that you may be filled with all the fulness of God" (Ephesians 3:19).

# CHAPTER FOURTEEN: "IN THE NAME" AND "INTO THE NAME" (GEOFF HYDON)

Some little phrases found in our Bible pass us by with little of our attention devoted to understanding them. In fact they can be full of meaning. 'In the Name' is the first one two of them that we are going to take a closer look at.

**Things that Differ**

As a starting point we need to distinguish between things that differ; although our English Bibles often do not differentiate between similar Greek words used by the original writers, differences do exist - even in respect to the little phrase we are focusing on now. The first thing to note is the difference between phrases which in the original writings use the Greek word en and those that use the word eis. The former is the general word meaning 'in' whereas the latter has more of the meaning of our word 'into'. Even in our everyday English we sometimes use these words almost interchangeably; yet there is a difference, as we shall see. Also, in some of the Greek expressions the definite article, usually translated 'the', is missing, but it is uniformly inserted in the English versions as a requirement of the English language. Do these apparently minor differences have any bearing on how we should understand the writer's words? Certainly!

**In the Name ...**

Many of the phrases where the words 'in (rather than 'into') the Name of the Lord' are used, clearly fit into the category which means simply 'taking action by the authority of the Lord' (Acts 3:6; 1 Corinthians

5:4; James 5:10,14). We do not use the phrase 'in the name of' in that way very much today. An illustrative expression which comes most easily to mind is the command, 'Stop, in the name of the law!' Policemen may sometimes use that expression, for they act not under their own authority, but under the powers received from the state as law officers. It is relatively easy to see that use of a person's name implies using that person's authority; we bind ourselves by signing documents – our name on the document means we are responsible for the contents. So authority and responsibility are linked together when we use our name to get something done. Moreover, we can delegate our authority to others, so that on our behalf they may sign in our name. There are also plenty of examples of what is called 'namedropping'. This expression refers to the mention of a more important name than our own in order to obtain treatment we would expect that important person to receive. These mundane examples help us to see something of the Scriptural use of the term, 'In the Name of the Lord' (see Mark 9:41, 2 Thessalonians 3:6 and 2 Timothy 2:19). The phrase requires three things to be true:

1) The action taken or commanded is an action that the Lord wants to be done;

2) The Lord has the authority to require the action to be done;

3) The Lord is accountable for the results of the action taken in His Name.

Having arrived at this understanding, it is important to note the application of these requirements in the matter of prayer. We have no licence to ask God the Father for things that the Lord does not want us to have when we pray 'in His Name' (John 16:23). We should be aware from Scripture of the things that the Lord authorizes, and for these things we should pray. When we ask for what the Lord wants, we can rely on Him to provide for our need, because He makes Himself accountable for such things. This kind of faithful use of the Lord's authority is also illustrated for us in the words of Peter, when he commanded the lame man to walk 'in the Name of Jesus Christ' (Acts 3:6), and of Paul, when he commanded the evil spirit to depart from the soothsaying girl (Acts 16:18). At the same moment, such words are both a command to others and an appeal to the power of God. How many of our prayers truly warrant such an appeal to God?

As we continue to examine the force of the term 'In the Name of the Lord Jesus Christ', it is important for us to note that Christians are people who have surrendered their will to Christ; He is their Master and Lord. As such, they retain virtually no authority of their own; they should always act in accordance with His desire and upon His command. That is implicit in the use of the phrase 'in His Name'. Therefore, the Scripture speaks of "always giving thanks for all things in the Name of our Lord Jesus Christ to God, even the Father" (Ephesians 5:20), and "whatever you do in word or deed, do all in the Name of the Lord Jesus, giving thanks through to God the Father through Him" (Colossians 3:17). At first glance that might seem an unattainable standard, and no doubt it would be if it were not for the fact of God's provision of a new nature, the indwelling Holy Spirit and the instruction of the Word of God, to help us.

God's provision to meet the needs of believers in Christ is abundantly apparent at the time of their new birth. They are baptized by Christ into the Church which is His Body, and they receive the Holy Spirit (John 1:33; 1 Corinthians 12:13) who gifts each one with special ability (1 Corinthians 12:7); moreover, the fellowship of believers brings together a full complement of gifts to meet the needs of all (Ephesians 4:16). This is clearly the divine ideal. We do not always see it in practice; why is that? One fundamental reason is that fellowship of believers can only truly be achieved through mutual obedience to the authority of the Lord Jesus Christ. Although the immediate context of

Matthew 18:20 is the matter of judgement, it contains a very important statement of principle.

**Into the Name**

No doubt millions of people have heard the phrase, 'into the Name ...' used as Christian disciples are baptized. However, the significance of this little phrase can easily be lost. Our familiarity with expressions such as this one often leads us to pass them over without thinking just why they are used. This is especially the case when the expression sounds simple. What is the meaning of this little phrase?

'In the Name' carries the thought of acting upon Christ's authority, as we have seen, but what is the added significance of using 'into' instead of 'in'? If 'in' refers to the location of the authority used, then 'into' refers to moving from outside that sphere of authority to within it. Significantly, most of the New Testament occurrences (e.g. Matthew 28:19; Acts 8:16, 19:5, 1 Corinthians 1:13) of the use of the Greek expression literally translated 'into the Name' are in the context of baptism of a believer in water. This is done to testify to the disciple's obedience to Christ. The expression is also used in John 3:18 where it is clear that disbelief is equivalent to disobedience (see v.36); it is perhaps unnecessary to add that the gospel is presented to sinners for their obedience, not just their grudging acceptance (c.f. 2 Thessalonians 1:8; Hebrews 5:9). The believer's baptism, therefore, is intended to show that whereas in the past the person was not in subjection to Christ, they have now taken a position under His lordship.

A suitable analogy would be a soldier changing sides during a battle, leaving the command of one for the leadership of another. In that case, the change in direction would obviously be noticeable. Moreover, the absolute authority of the new commander would have to be acknowledged. Perhaps something of this thought is present in Paul's reference to Christ leading us in triumph: we are now subject to the leadership of

Christ instead of our former unsaved condition, where we were subject to the working of the 'principalities and powers', evil forces to whom we effectively subjected ourselves.

Where the definite article is present, the phrase helps to draw attention to the distinctive name in question: the name, not just any name. The significance of that is apparent from 1 Corinthians 1:13,15 where the whole issue rests upon into whose name the disciples were baptized; Peter and Paul should not be treated on the same plane as Christ. Paul is therefore saying the Name that matters is Christ's, and the superiority of that Name is emphasized by using the little word 'the'.

The authority of God the Father, the lordship of God the Son and the leadership of God the Holy Spirit are all combined in the Name, not Names, into which the believer is baptized. That is, the believer is evidencing submission to God the Three-in-One in baptism. The use of the singular, 'Name' (Matthew 28:19) emphasizes the essential equality of each of the Persons of the Godhead. This is most important. In early days, just as today, many were not ready to give Christ any higher estimation than that of a good man or a prophet. But the words used at a believer's baptism give Christ His true place as God the Son. If people were baptized simply into the Name of Jesus, then it might appear to be no more than some in Corinth seemed to view it: evidence of discipleship to a man, like Paul or Peter. Linking together in the one Name the three Persons of the Godhead establishes the right of the Lord Jesus Christ to rule in the believer's life, for in this respect there is no-one with greater authority than He. It is no surprise, therefore, that such authority was claimed by Christ before He gave His command to the apostles to make and baptize disciples (Matthew 28:19). In later commands to baptize, the title Lord is used, and we can immediately see that the deity of Christ is well expressed in that tide.

The Lord's command to baptize was both a continuity and a progression in His teaching. During the days of His ministry, He had taught His disciples to baptize converts. In this respect we can safely presume two features of such baptism:

> (1) It was of the same character as the baptism of John; it was a sign of repentance and done as preparation for salvation (which Christ Himself was later to accomplish).
>
> (2) It did not necessarily involve those baptized witnessing to a belief in Jesus as Son of God. This seems apparent from the fact that such baptism pre-dated Peter's climactic declaration of the deity of Christ (John 4:1,2; Matthew 16:13-21). Despite John the Baptist's words, it seems that many saw Messiah as from God, but not as God.

The Lord's commands to His apostles on the mountain in Galilee would therefore continue their previous practice of baptizing disciples, but add a marked progressive change. Henceforward, the deity of the resurrected Lord was to be explicit in the baptism of disciples. The little word 'into' is so necessary to evidence submission to that lordship, and the Name of the Trinity acknowledges the deity of the Lord Jesus Christ.

From what has been said, it is clear that the use of the term '... into the Name ...' at the time of a believer's baptism is not intended to be mere ritual language; it is expressive of the essential condition, without which such a baptism would be inappropriate and pointless. Having left behind thoughts of self-determination, the believer in submitting to baptism is evidencing a distinctive change in leadership. The baptism is intended to be a clear statement of acknowledging Christ's lordship, and therefore of the believer's willingness to be submissive to His commands. Such submission was a necessary part of the act of faith which results in salvation.

## THE NAME OF JESUS

Jesus! that name all names above

Sweet passport of eternal love,

Unfolding to a fallen race

The wealth of God's infinite grace.

What mind can grasp, what tongue proclaim

The value of that peerless name?

Jesus! a note of sweeter sound

Not e'en in heaven itself is found;

It thrills with joy the heart of God,

This name of the incarnate Word.

What mind can grasp, what tongue proclaim

The sweetness of that peerless name?

Jesus! the name that ne'er can fail

To make the powers of darkness quail;

To fear-wrung heart give lasting peace,

Sin-burdened souls complete release.

What mind can grasp, what tongue proclaim

The prowess of that peerless name?

Jesus! the name which can impart

True solace to each sorrowing heart;

Of death subdue the sting and gloom,

With heavenly glory gild the tomb.

What mind can grasp, what tongue proclaim

The comfort of that peerless name?

Jesus! the name through which alone

Believing ones approach the throne;

To God their hearts' desires outpour

And draw from heaven's exhaustless store.

What mind can grasp, what tongue proclaim

The riches of that peerless name?

Jesus! the name in which shall bow

Each knee in heaven, on earth below;

God glorify with one accord,

Confessing Jesus Christ as Lord.

May we each day by day proclaim

The glory of that peerless name.

And when we pass to realms above,

See Him who taught us heavenly love,

With ransomed hosts enraptured raise

Triumphant songs of ceaseless praise,

Unhindered then shall we proclaim

The virtues of that peerless name!

(R. Murray)

# CHAPTER FIFTEEN: REDEEMER (GEORGE PRASHER)

There is a special sweetness to the Christian's heart about the thought of Christ as Redeemer. As the hymn writer has written:

"My Redeemer! oh what beauties

In that lovely Name appear!

None but Jesus in His glories

Shall the honoured title wear.

My Redeemer, My Redeemer!

Thou hast my salvation wrought"

The Greek words translated "redeem" in our Bibles have the thought of "buying out" (as when buying a slave with a view to freedom), and of releasing on payment of a ransom. They convey the idea of deliverance which could never be achieved apart from intervention by one who is willing and able to save.

A great Bible illustration of redemption is the deliverance of the nation of Israel from Egypt in the time of Moses. On the night of the Passover, a nation of slaves was released to freedom. The blood of a slain lamb on their doorposts had sheltered them from the destroying angel: and the impact of the death of the firstborn son in countless Egyptian homes made the tyrant Pharaoh urge the Hebrews to leave his land. Their mighty exodus from Egypt and through the Red Sea brought complete deliverance. They were redeemed by divine power, God destroyed the pursuing Egyptian army and set His people free.

## SPARKLING FACETS: BIBLE NAMES AND TITLES OF JESUS

And we have known redemption, Lord,

From bondage worse than theirs by far;

Sin held us by a stronger cord,

Yet by Thy mercy free we are.

These words of the hymn writer turn our thoughts to the excellence of the One through whom we have been redeemed from Satan's power. He is described in Ephesians 1 as "the Beloved" in whom we have our redemption through His blood, the forgiveness of our trespasses, through the riches of His grace (vv.6,7). Yes, our Redeemer is none other than God's own beloved Son. Our redemption is through His blood, because the power of Satan and of sin could never have been broken if our Redeemer had not dealt with the problem of sin. This could only be by His death for our sake.

"Being justified freely by His grace through the redemption that is in Christ Jesus, whom God set forth as a propitiation by His blood, through faith ..." (Romans 3:24,25). So Jesus bore in His own Person the judgement for sinners on the cross. He completely satisfied all God's claims against the sinner through His one sacrifice for sins forever. He gave Himself a ransom for all (1 Timothy 2:6). As a result of this our faith in the Saviour brings us redemption and deliverance.

By weakness and defeat

He won the meed and crown;

Trod all our foes beneath His feet

By being trodden down.

There is a glorious ring of triumph in the words of Hebrews 9:12: "... through His own blood, entered in once for all into the holy place, having obtained eternal redemption." Let us enjoy fully the assurance of these words - eternal redemption! This derives from the perfect sacrifice of our Redeemer at Calvary: He Himself is the Guarantor of our redemption, as He lives in the power of an endless life.

Some aspects of Christ's work as Redeemer are remarkably foreshadowed in the Old Testament. For instance, if through poverty an Israelite had to sell himself to a stranger, God's Law laid the responsibility of redeeming him upon a near kinsman, a close relation. That faintly illustrates the truth that in order to redeem us, the Lord Jesus had to become our kinsman. In a very special sense He did so, by partaking of flesh and blood and through His birth of the virgin; being found here in this world in fashion as a man.

Another requirement of the Law of Moses was that the firstborn of an ass had to have its neck broken unless it was redeemed by the death of a lamb in its place. The ass was classified as an unclean animal. On countless occasions, therefore, in Israel's history, if the owner of an ass wanted its firstborn to live, the life of a lamb had to be given in its place, so there was repeatedly enacted the giving of the clean for the unclean. As men obeyed this requirement of God's Law, they were expressing before Him one great truth of His redemptive purpose - that in due time the Holy One of God, the spotless lamb, would yield His life to make possible the redemption of a race defiled by sin. How thankful we should feel for this! That gratitude should find expression in a willingness to respond to God's purpose in our redemption.

Paul wrote about that great purpose for which Christ gave Himself a ransom in his letter to Titus: "... who gave Himself for us, that He might redeem us from every lawless deed, and purify for Himself His own special people, zealous of good works" (Titus 2:14). Holiness of life should be seen in every redeemed person. But more than that, disciples should be united together as a people for His pleasure, a people marked out by their zeal for good works.

God's purpose in our redemption does not stop there! Holiness in our Christian experience is an important result which should be seen. But we are also eagerly awaiting our adoption, the redemption of our bodies (Romans 8:23). At present we may glorify God in our bodies, but they are subject to imperfection and disease; and how well we know the power of the law of sin in our members! These problems cause us to "groan within ourselves, waiting for ... the redemption of our body". When will this take place? It will take place when the Lord Jesus returns for His Church. Paul wrote about this in his letter to the Philippians: "... we wait for a Saviour, the Lord Jesus Christ: who shall fashion anew the body of our humiliation, that it may be conformed to the body of His glory, according to the working whereby He is able even to subject all things unto Himself" (Philippians 3:20,21).

So our great Redeemer will bring this purpose to completion. At present we have to endure the problems of a mortal body and a sinful environment. These very problems may prove to be a means of our more fully glorifying God through overcoming faith. Our Redeemer also promises us the redemption of our body - to be conformed to His own glorious body! Wonderful Redeemer!

Sunk in ruin, sin and misery,

Bound by Satan's captive chain

Guided by his artful treachery,

Hurrying on to endless pain;

My Redeemer

Plucked me as a brand from hell

Mine for time and mine for ever

Mine by oath and mine by blood,

Mine, nor time the bond shall sever

Mine as the unchanging God,

My Redeemer!

Oh, how sweet to call Him mine!

When in heaven I see Thy glory,

When before Thy throne I bow,

Perfectly I shall be like Thee,

Fully Thy redemption know,

My Redeemer

Then shall hear me shout His praise.

(Author Unknown)

# CHAPTER SIXTEEN: HEAD OF THE CHURCH (GEORGE PRASHER)

To believers in the Lord Jesus during this present age of grace, there is a special appeal about His excellency as Head of the Church which is His Body. The divine purpose in the Body of Christ is unique to the present age. Since the day of Pentecost following the Lord's resurrection, the gospel of the grace of God has reached countless hearts. All who have believed its message are members of the Body of Christ: this gives some idea of the vastness of the Church which is His Body. Most of its members are already in heaven with Christ, having died as believers in Him. But every born-again believer in the world today is also a member of the Body.

To realize the immense numbers included in the Church the Body impresses on us the majesty and splendour of this divine purpose. Equally it helps us to appreciate the dignity of Christ's position and title as Head of the Church. Indeed in Ephesians chapter 1 this is directly related to His supremacy. For God:

> "raised Him from the dead, and made Him to sit at His right hand in the heavenly places, far above all rule ... and power and dominion, and every name that is named, not only in this world, but also in that which is to come: and He put all things in subjection under His feet, and gave Him to be Head over all things to the Church, which is His Body, the fulness of Him that filleth all in all" (Ephesians 1:20-23).

A similar emphasis on His Headship of the Body as reflecting Christ's supremacy is also seen in Colossians chapter 1:

"And He is before all things, and in Him all things consist. And He is the Head of the Body the Church: who is the beginning, the firstborn from the dead; that in all things He might have the preeminence. For it was the good pleasure of the Father that in Him should all the fulness dwell" (vv.17-19).

So the position of our Lord Jesus Christ as the Head of the Church renews to our hearts today the glory of His exaltation, the fact that He is the head of all principality and power. Thinking a little further of the scripture in Ephesians chapter 1 you will remember that it says that God put all things in subjection under Christ's feet, and gave Him to be Head over all things to the Church which is His Body. It is not, in this context, that the Church is given to Him, but that He is given to the Church. He is Head over all things, but He is given to the Church to be Head over it also. So gloriously honoured are all who have become members of the Body through faith in Him.

Yet there is also the remarkable statement that the Church is the fulness of Him that filleth all in all; or the fulness of Him who fills everything in every way, as one version puts it: The word translated "fulness" means that which fills or complements. So the great company of the redeemed who form the Church are complementary to Christ: They reflect the glory of His grace in what He has made them, an answer to the desires of His heart.

But supreme authority in exaltation is only one excellence of Christ seen in His Headship of the Church the Body. Ephesians chapter 5 also brings out the beauty of His love for the Church: "Christ also loved the Church, and gave Himself up for it" (v.25). We believers, as members of His Body, marvel that One so great should have given Himself at Calvary to make possible our eternal union with Him. R.C. Chapman wrote in one of his hymns:

The Head for all the members

The curse, the vengeance bore,

And God, our God remembers

His people's sins no more.

Again we read, "Christ also is the Head of the Church, being Himself the Saviour of the Body" (Ephesians 5:23). The word "saviour" in this verse may be better understood in the sense of "preserver". The Lord Jesus, almighty Head of the Church, preserves those He has saved, guarding each member in indissoluble union with Himself, the Head. Wonderful and eternal security in Him!

Then He is also the Sanctifier of the Church: "That He might sanctify it, having cleansed it by the washing of water by the Word" (Ephesians 5:26). In giving Himself for the Church Christ had in view that it might be to Him what it can never be to any other. Just as in God's ideal of marriage, the husband regards the wife as set apart to him, so that she can be to him what none other can. All this is with the intention of presenting the Church to Himself a glorious Church, without spot or wrinkle or any such thing: but that it should be holy and without blemish. She will be all glorious, He is her Head, her Creator, her Builder, her Saviour, her Sanctifier and her Cleanser. He will be as her Husband and she His Bride.

Let us enjoy the thought of our assured place as members of His Body in that eternal and glorious relationship with Him. What is true of the whole Church is true of you and me as individual members of His Body. We shall be without spot or wrinkle. The spot or stain indicates sin: the wrinkle a fault or blemish or the effect of age. But we shall each be lifted above all such effects of sin and human frailty. We shall share His unsullied holiness when the Church is presented to her heavenly Bridegroom. And all this springs from the fact that Christ loved the

Church and gave Himself for her. He will then see of the travail of His soul and be satisfied. Our hearts also thrill to the thought of that coming triumph, and we gladly echo Charles Wesley's appreciation of it:

Head of the Church triumphant,

Now seated in the glory!

Till He appear His members here,

O God would bow before Thee.

Head of the Church triumphant!

We lift our hearts and voices

In blest anticipation, and cry aloud,

And give to God the praise of our salvation.

By faith we see the glory

Of which Thou dost assure us

The world despise for that high prize

Which Thou has set before us,

We wait with expectation

The happy consumation

Of His blest promise given,

To meet our Lord, by all adored

And swell the praise of heaven.

# CHAPTER SEVENTEEN: THE FIRSTBORN (GEORGE PRASHER)

There are four references to Christ as the Firstborn in our New Testament:

1) Firstborn among many brethren (Romans 8:29)

2) Firstborn of all creation (Colossians 1:15)

3) Firstborn from the dead (Colossians 1:18)

4) Firstborn of the dead (Revelation 1:5).

What is implied by this word Firstborn? It is a title of honour, and it indicates one who has precedence, who occupies the highest place. It is derived, of course, from its use in connection with families, for the firstborn in a family had a special privilege and honour. It is sometimes used, however, where no family relationship exists. For example, God said of David: "I also will make him My firstborn, the highest of the kings of the earth" (Psalm 89:27).

Another such example is its use in Colossians 1:15, where the Lord Jesus is described as "the image of the invisible God, the Firstborn of all creation". In the same context we are also told that in Him were all things created. So the title does not involve the thought of the Lord Jesus having a beginning. He who is "the image of the invisible God" is Himself truly God. John tells us plainly that, "the Word was God" (John 1:1). The statements made in Hebrews chapter 1 concerning the Son are very definite: "Thy throne, O God, is for ever and ever ... Thou, Lord, in the beginning hast laid the foundation of the earth ..." (vv. 8,10).

The title "Firstborn" does not refer to His being the Son of the Father, for in that sense He was not the first, but the only begotten Son (John 3:16). Christ, as Firstborn, is the One who occupies the position of dignity, precedence and priority over all creation, as shown by the words: "... the Firstborn of all creation; for in Him were all things created, all things have been created through Him, and unto Him; and He is before all things, and in Him all things consist ... who is the beginning, the Firstborn from the dead; that in all things He might have the preeminence" (Colossians 1:15-18).

As to His being the Firstborn from the dead, this marks Him out as having preeminence in relation to all others who share in resurrection. In Ephesians chapter 1 we are given a tremendous impression of the mighty power exerted in the resurrection of the Lord Jesus, and of His unique exaltation:

> "According to that working of the strength of His might which He wrought in Christ when He raised Him from the dead, and made Him to sit at His right hand in the heavenly places, far above all rule, and authority, and power, and dominion, and every name that is named, not only in this world, but also in that which is to come; and He put all things in subjection under His feet" (vv.20-22).

It is in the light of such words that we understand more fully the glory and honour due to the Lord Jesus as the Firstborn from the dead. We are also reminded of the glorious fact that because He lives we shall live also. Christ is described in 1 Corinthians 15 as "the first fruits of them that are asleep" (v.20). His resurrection is the beginning of an immense harvest: "For as in Adam all die, so also in Christ shall all be made alive. But each in his own order: Christ the first fruits; then they that are Christ's, at His coming" (1 Corinthians 15:22,23).

As believers in Him, we await the fulfilment of His promise given in the Upper Room before He went to the cross. "I come again, and will receive you unto Myself" (John 14:3). It is clear from 1 Thessalonians 4 that when He returns to the air for His Church, those who are alive and remain until the coming of the Lord will by no means precede those who have fallen asleep in Jesus. For the dead in Christ will rise first; they will be raised incorruptible, and those alive in mortal bodies at His coming will put on immortality for we shall all be changed. Then shall be brought to pass the saying, "Death is swallowed up in victory". The hymn writer has reflected the triumph of this hope when she wrote;

True, the silent grave is keeping

Many a seed in weakness sown,

But the saints in Thee now sleeping,

Raised in power shall share Thy throne,

Resurrection!

Lord of glory, 'tis Thine own.

And another hymn writer, John Wesley, wrote these words:

First-born of many brethren Thou,

To whom both heaven and earth must bow

Heirs of Thy shame and of Thy throne

We bear the cross and seek the crown.

# CHAPTER EIGHTEEN: LORD AND CHRIST (GEORGE PRASHER)

In the prophet Isaiah's generation there were those who "put darkness for light, and light for darkness" (Isaiah 5:20) and who turned things upside down (Isaiah 29:16). We hear the same order of reasoning today regarding the Person of our Lord Jesus Christ. The Lord Himself did not claim to be God, the argument runs; this idea was developed later among His disciples who attributed to Him more than He claimed for Himself. Turning things upside down indeed! For the truth of the Deity and Messiahship of the Lord Jesus was declared through the prophets of the Old Testament, and He endorsed the application of those prophecies to Himself as related in the gospels. Moreover, His ministry confirmed from other viewpoints that He was both Lord and Christ. Let us first consider three Old Testament prophecies to which the Lord Jesus referred in such a way that they confirm His Deity and Messiahship.

When discussing the quality of John the Baptist's character and ministry in Luke 7, the Lord asked: "... what did you go out to see? A man dressed in fine clothes? No, those who wear expensive clothes and indulge in luxury are in palaces. But what did you go out to see? A prophet? Yes, I tell you, and more than a prophet. This is the one about whom it is written: "'I will send my messenger ahead of you, who will prepare your way before you" (Luke 7:24,26,27 NIV; cf. Malachi 3:1).

The verse in Malachi makes clear that the messenger was to prepare the way before the Lord. By applying Malachi's words to John the Baptist, the Lord Jesus was confirming that He was the divine Person who would come suddenly to His temple. There is a parallel in Isaiah 40:3 in the description of John the Baptist's ministry - A voice of one calling: "In the wilderness prepare the way for the Lord (Jehovah); make straight in the desert a highway for our God" (Elohim) (NIV). Although the gospel writers do not record the Lord Jesus as applying these prophetic words to the Baptist, the Holy Spirit moved the three synoptic gospel writers to apply the prophecy in this way. If we accept Scripture to be God's inspired word, it follows that Isaiah ascribes to the Lord Jesus both the name Jehovah and the name Elohim.

As the Lord was giving instruction to two of His disciples about the colt on which He would ride into Jerusalem, we are told in Matthew's gospel that He added "all this was done that it might be fulfilled which was spoken by the prophet, saying: "Tell the daughter of Zion, 'Behold, your King is coming to you, Lowly, and sitting on a donkey, A colt, the foal of a donkey'" (Matthew 21:4,5).

Who was this King of whom Zechariah prophesied? (Zechariah 9:9). "He shall speak peace to the nations; His dominion shall be from sea to sea, and from the River to the ends of the earth" (verse 10). Only one King can be identified to answer to this description - "the LORD of hosts", who "shall reign on Mount Zion, and in Jerusalem, and before His elders gloriously" (Isaiah 24:23). In applying Zechariah's prophecy to Himself, the Lord Jesus was again declaring both His Deity and Messiahship.

Question after question had been devised by Pharisee, Sadducee and scribe in their efforts to gain advantage over the Lord Jesus. But on every occasion His answers silenced them, for "never man so spake". Matthew 22:42 records that He asked the Pharisees what they thought of the Christ, and they replied that He was the son of David. "He said to them, 'How then does David in the Spirit call Him 'Lord,' saying: 'The Lord said to my Lord, "Sit at My right hand, Till I make Your enemies Your footstool"'?If David then calls Him 'Lord,' how is He his

Son?" And no one was able to answer Him a word, nor from that day on did anyone dare question Him anymore."

However, the Lord's use of this quote from Psalm 110 is explained by the Holy Spirit in Hebrews 1:13. There David's Lord is identified as the Lord Jesus Christ, to whom God has said, "Sit at my My right hand, till I make Your enemies Your footstool". The Lord Jesus was David's son in that He was born of the seed of David according to the flesh; but He was also David's Lord as the Son of God from everlasting. He was both the Root and the Offspring of David. His question from Psalm 110 resounds with the truth of His Deity.

"Why does this man speak blasphemies like this? Who can forgive sins but God alone?" (Mark 2:7). This was the indignant response of certain of the scribes when the Lord said to a paralysed man, "Your sins are forgiven". The man had been lowered through the roof of the house in which the Lord was teaching. Dealing with the patient's deepest need first, the Saviour assured him of forgiveness of sins. Immediately this was challenged, because only God can forgive sins. The Lord deliberately took up the challenge: "Why do you reason about these things in your hearts?" He asked. "But that you may know that the Son of Man has power on earth to forgive sins' - He said to the paralytic), 'I say to you, arise, take up your bed, and go to your house".

The divine power which immediately healed the paralysed man demonstrated the Lord's authority to forgive sins. Little wonder "they were all amazed, and glorified God, saying, We never saw anything like this". For ourselves we see in His authority to forgive sins the Lord's further confirmation of His Deity. His exercise of this divine prerogative was seen again in His dealings with the sinner woman of Luke 7: "Your sins are forgiven ... your faith has saved you. Go in peace" (verses 48-50).

Many of the Jews who listened to the ministry of the Lord Jesus took strong exception to His references to God as His Father. As explained in John 5:18: "For this reason therefore the Jews sought all the more to kill Him, because He not only broke the Sabbath, but also said that God was His Father, making Himself equal with God". Were they simply misunderstanding what the Lord Jesus meant by calling God His own Father? If that had been so, the Lord would have corrected them and denied any claim to equality with God. Far from doing this He emphasized time and again the uniqueness of His relationship with the Father:

> "For the Father loves the Son, and shows Him all things that He Himself does; and He will show Him greater works than these, that you may marvel. For as the Father raises the dead and gives life to them, even so the Son gives life to whom He will. For the Father judges no one, but has committed all judgment to the Son, that all should honor the Son just as they honor the Father. He who does not honor the Son does not honor the Father who sent Him" (John 5:20-23).

It was at the feast of the dedication at Jerusalem that He declared: "I and my Father are one". This prompted the Jews to take up stones again to stone Him. Asked for which of the good works shown from the Father they wished to stone Him, they answered: "For a good work we do no stone You, but for blasphemy; and because You, being a man, make Yourself God" (John 10:30-33). Again on this occasion there was no withdrawal by the Lord Jesus of what He had said. Rather He reminded them that even men (the elders of Israel) to whom God's word came were described as "gods" (Psalm 82:6). How much more should He, whom the Father had sanctified and sent into the world, be called "the Son of God"? Again He appealed to the works given Him by the Father as evidence that He was in the Father and the Father in Him (John 10:38).

It seems remarkable that when Peter so clearly confessed the Lord Jesus to be "the Christ, the Son of the living God", the disciples were charged that they should tell no man who He was (Matthew 16:16,20). Nor were Peter, James and John to tell anyone about their experience on the Mount of Transfiguration until the Son of Man had been raised from the dead. The truth of the Lord's Deity and Messiahship pervaded His ministry, but could only be understood by those with earnest spiritual concern, to whom the Father in heaven would reveal it. It could not be humanly apprehended. The natural mind tended to view the hope of Messiah's earthly kingdom as the answer to the political situation of that time. A Christ of earthly glory and worldwide power was their expectation. They remained blind to the fulfilment in the Lord Jesus of the prophetic truth regarding Jehovah's Servant, the suffering Christ. They saw in Him no beauty that they should desire Him. "Shall their want of faith make of no effect the faithfulness of God? God forbid!" In His earthly ministry the Faithful Witness left no doubt that He was "both Lord and Christ".

# CHAPTER NINETEEN: THE JUDGE (GEORGE PRASHER)

How thankful we should be that God did not send His Son into the world to judge the world, but that the world should be saved through Him! The Lord Jesus Himself said: "And if any man hears My words, and does not believe, I do not judge him: for I did not come to judge the world, but to save the world" (John 12:47).

God has, however, appointed a day in which He will judge the world in righteousness by the Man whom He has ordained, our Lord Jesus Christ: and the certainty of this has been confirmed by the Lord's resurrection from the dead. The Lord Jesus Himself said: "For the Father judges no-one, but has committed all judgement to the Son; that all should honour the Son, just as they honour the Father" (John 5:22,23). So the Lord Jesus will be the executor of all divine judgement. Let us think for a moment about one of the Lord's most reassuring promises. It can be found in John 5:24: "Most assuredly, I say to you, he who hears My word and believes in Him who sent Me has everlasting life, and shall not come into judgment, but has passed from death into life."

We trust that each one of us who has accepted Christ as Saviour is resting thankfully in the assurance of this wonderful promise. It confirms the finality of our salvation from the judgement of God. When we believed on the Lord Jesus Christ we passed out of death into life. Because His sacrifice at Calvary for our sins was perfectly completed, each believer is saved from the wrath of God through Him.

But are not all believers told in the epistles to the Romans and to the Corinthians that we must all stand before the judgement seat of Christ? Yes, that is so, but we must distinguish between that judgement and the judgement to be experienced by the unbeliever. The reference to the judgement seat of Christ in Romans 14:10 is in relation to the believer's attitude to his brethren - the possibility of wrongly judging another's actions or motives. "Why do you judge your brother?", Paul asks, and then he solemnly reminds us that, "We shall all stand before the judgement seat of Christ", inferring that these are things that should be left to the Lord to judge.

There is a similar emphasis in 1 Corinthians 4:1-5, where the apostle discusses our stewardship of the truths of the Faith: "Therefore judge nothing before the time, until the Lord comes, who will both bring to light the hidden things of darkness, and reveal the counsels of the hearts. Then each one's praise shall come from God" (v.5).

Of course there are other matters upon which disciples of the Lord Jesus are responsible to form a judgement, such as the need to discipline an evildoer as in the Corinthian Church (see 1 Corinthians 5:1-13). So the believer's appearing before the judgement seat of Christ will be for the assessment of his service, to receive the things done in the body according to what we have done whether it be good or bad. Referring to his own service Paul wrote: "I have kept the Faith. Finally, there is laid up for me the crown of righteousness, which the Lord, the righteous Judge will give to me on that Day" (2 Timothy 4:7,8).

When will "that day" be? We would understand that believers of this age will appear before the judgement seat of Christ immediately following His coming to the air to take His saints from the world. This seems to be confirmed in Revelation chapter 19 where we read: "The marriage of the Lamb is come, and His wife hath made herself ready. And it was given unto her that she should array herself in fine line, bright and pure: for the fine linen is the righteous acts of the saints" (vv.7,8). From which it would seem that the saints of this present dispensation will have already been before the judgement seat of Christ.

Their works have been assessed by Him, their righteous acts are seen as fine linen, bright and pure. Following this, the Lord Jesus is portrayed as King of kings and Lord of lords, coming to earth to take His great power and reign. The nations of the earth will at that time be judged by Him, as illustrated in the parable of the sheep and the goats (Matthew 25:31-46).

The final great assize will not take place until the end of His thousand-year reign: that will be at the awesome judgement of the Great White Throne as described in Revelation chapter 20. All who have not shared in the earlier phases of resurrection will then be raised from the dead to be judged by Him there. The great and the small will stand before the Throne. They will be judged out of the things written in the books, according to their works - marvellous divine records of myriad human lives! Another book too will be opened - the book of life. We understand that many standing before the Great White Throne for judgement will find their names written in the book of life.

For millions have lived and died without hearing the gospel of Christ - among them are many such as are described in Romans chapter 2 who by "patient continuance in doing good seek for glory, honor, and immortality". They will be judged according to their works because these reflected spiritual light was available to them. Their guilt as sinners before God will be covered by Christ's work at Calvary. On this ground their names will be found in the book of life.

"But to those who are self-seeking and do not obey the truth, but obey unrighteousness - indignation and wrath, tribulation and anguish, on every soul of man who does evil" (Romans 2:8,9). So wrote Paul as he discoursed on God's dealings with men. The word of God solemnly confirms that at the judgement of the Great White Throne, Death and Hades were cast into the lake of fire. This is the second death, even the lake of fire. And if any was not found written in the book of life, he was cast into the lake of fire (Revelation 20:14,15).

We naturally recoil from the thought of such fearful judgement: But we realize that the One who sits upon the Throne, from whose face heaven and earth flee away, is the same One whose face was marred more than any man's on Calvary's cross. All who hear the verdict against them on that day will have chosen judgement by their rejection of all God's pleadings that they should turn to Him and receive His mercy. When we know as we are known, when we are with the Lord and like Him, we shall see everything in a clearer light: We shall join the acclaim of the great multitude in heaven, of which we read in Revelation chapter 19: "Salvation, and glory, and honour and power belong to the Lord our God: for true and righteous are His judgements ..." (vv.1,2).

Meantime, resting by faith on God's word, we share the confidence expressed by Abraham, when God was about to visit judgement on Sodom and Gomorrah: "Shall not the Judge of all the earth do right?" (Genesis 18:25).

# CHAPTER TWENTY: THE LAST ADAM (BRIAN JOHNSTON)

References to Adam and Eve by the Lord in His public ministry confirm that the early accounts of the book of Genesis are to be taken as historical narrative. Adam was therefore literally the first man. Scripture reveals God's overall plan for creation in terms of two men: "the first man Adam" also called "the first man"; and "the last Adam" or "the Second Man" (1 Corinthians 15:45,47). Adam is presented as the head of the first creation and Christ as the head of the new creation. In this way, Adam can be seen as a striking type of Christ. He is, in fact, the only person declared explicitly in Scripture to be a type of Christ ("figure", Greek: tupos, Romans 5:14). Different aspects of Adam as a type of Christ in the divine purpose are reviewed below.

**First man of earth; second man of heaven**

In Genesis 2:7 we are plainly told that "the LORD God formed man of the dust of the ground, and breathed into his nostrils the breath of life; and man became a living soul". By breaking God's command and eating of the tree concerning which God had commanded him not to eat, Adam was rendered mortal, that is his body became subject to death. This mortality was to be transmitted to his descendants: "as in Adam all die, so also in Christ shall all be made alive" (1 Corinthians 15:22). It is in the context of bodily resurrection that we go on to read in verse 45: "the first man Adam became a living soul. The last Adam became a life-giving spirit," this latter having specific regard to the making alive of the bodies of dead believers at the Lord's coming again.

God told Adam that, after the Fall, work would become onerous "till thou return unto the ground; for out of it wast thou taken: for dust thou art, and unto dust shalt thou return" (Genesis 3:19). The psalmists remind us of this: "Thou turnest man to dust; and sayest, Return, ye children of men" (Psalm 90:3 Revised Version Margin): "For He knoweth our frame; He remembereth that we are dust" (Psalm 103:14). The earthen vessel, having thus become marred, required renewing in God's image (Colossians 3:10). This was to be accomplished through the work of the Second Man, the promised seed.

As to the Second Man, it is Matthew who declares the virgin birth of the Lord Jesus to be in direct fulfilment of the Isaiah prophecy (Isaiah 7:14). The interpretation of the name given to the child is the interpretation of the event itself: God with us. Isaiah also had stated (in Isaiah 9:6) that the child born was to be identified as the Son given. And so the Second Man, the antitype of the first, is revealed in Scripture as being the Lord from heaven. In the case of the first man, as we have noted above, we are dealing with the great creation miracle of man being made after God's likeness (Genesis 1:26); but when we consider the Second Man, a far greater wonder unfolds, namely, the incarnation miracle of deity becoming in the likeness of men (Philippians 2:7).

We cannot fail to be impressed with the accuracy of Romans 8:3 - "God, sending His own Son in the likeness of sinful flesh ..." How necessary are the words "likeness" and "sinful"! He who existed originally in the form of God, came to be found in fashion as a man. "Form" and "fashion" are contrasting words in Philippians 2:6,8. "Fashion" refers to an outward expression which is assumed; while "form" is representative of one's inmost being. Thus "form" has nothing to do with shape as we might assume from the English word, but as applied to the Lord it necessarily implies the possession of the divine essence.

The Lord never relinquished His deity in becoming man. He was always more than man. But through the incarnation He assumed humanity, becoming what He had never been before. Consider the practical implications of the same contrasting idea as applied to ourselves in the words "fashioned" and "transformed" of Romans 12:2. The former concerns an outward expression which is merely assumed, while the latter has in view one which is indicative of our new nature.

### The image of God

"God created man in His own image" (Genesis 1:27). Man's body itself did not involve a new creation, since it was formed out of the dust of the ground (Genesis 2:7), the basic elements of which had been created on the first day of creation. But when God created man in His own image, He called into being a distinct and eternal individual personality, capable of fellowship with Himself. Physical attributes, as well as biological, can be transmitted from parents to children by definite genetic laws. However, for each new person so generated, there is also a special creation which takes place, the "image of God", a unique and eternal personality, capable of fellowship with the Creator. This is not true of the animals, whose physical and biological characteristics are purely the result of heredity and environment. This sets man apart from the brute creation, for in the thought of "image", God created Adam as a visible representation of Himself. Pre-Fall, Adam was a perfect vehicle for the manifestation of such Godlike qualities as the ability to rule and make decisions and exercise a sense of responsibility as a moral being.

Paul, when writing to the Colossians of the supremacy of Christ, describes Him as the "image of the invisible God" (Colossians 1:15). The Lord Jesus Christ, the last Adam, is essentially and absolutely the perfect expression and representation of God the Father. He is the visible manifestation of God to created beings. He Himself could say that whoever had seen Him had seen the Father (John 14:9). It is worth noting in passing that it is a different word that is translated "image" and used of the Lord Jesus in Hebrews 1:3. There the idea is of the exact correspondence between the image on a die and the imprint it produces, for example in wax - teaching us that the Lord Jesus is personally distinct from and yet literally equal to God the Father.

**Head of creation; firstborn of all creation (Colossians 1:15).**

Adam was made, as God's representative, to head up creation. David, in Psalm 8 could say: "Thou madest him to have dominion over the works of Thy hands; Thou hast put all things under his feet: ... the beasts of the field ... the fowl of the air, and the fish of the sea" (vv. 6-8). The words of this Psalm have special significance for the Second Man (see 1 Corinthians 15:27; Hebrews 2:6-9). The Second Man, the last Adam, is God's preeminent One - "the Firstborn of all creation" (cf. Psalm 89:27). Praise be to God that the "Firstborn of all creation" (Colossians 1:15) became the "Firstborn from the dead" (Colossians 1:18) in order that He might become the "Firstborn among many brethren" (Romans 8:29).

**Comparisons and contrasts**

In Romans chapter 5 we have Adam pictured as the head of a race of sinful men and Christ at the head of a race of men who have been made righteous. The teaching of Romans chapter 5 for believers is that we were made sinful in the first Adam and made righteous in the last Adam; our new head. In both cases the personal acts of individuals as such are not in view, but it is the effect through imputation of the actions of each head on their respective race, and that by virtue of its solidarity with its head. As the argument passes from verse 12 to verse 18, we read: "through one man sin entered ... so death passed unto all men, for that all sinned ... as through one trespass the judgement came to all men to condemnation; even so through one act of righteousness ... justification of life".

We sinned in the first Adam, our old head, and this made us dead to God. As believers we then were seen as having died with Christ, the last

Adam, our new head, and so were made dead to sin and alive to God (Romans 6). The two key figures in God's framework are here presented side by side by the Spirit: Adam who in disobedience walked to the tree in the midst of the garden, and the Second Man who in obedience walked to the tree just outside Jerusalem.

In Paul's magnificent discourse of chapter 5, Adam is seen as having brought sin, condemnation, and death to his race through his disobedience. Christ, by glorious contrast, through His obedience has brought righteousness, justification, and life to the race of which He is head. Just as there was to be not only full restitution, but additionally an excess 20 per cent compensation in the case of the trespass offering (Leviticus 6), so we read that Christ's act of righteousness not only reverses the effects of Adam's trespass but, in the twice-repeated words of vv.15-17, it has achieved "much more" besides.

**Adam and Eve**

God officiated at the very first marriage as recorded in Genesis chapter 2. It was to the positive instruction of this original prototype that the Lord turned the minds of those who in His day were concerned with departures from it (Matthew 19:3-9). In marrying Adam to Eve, God not only presented us with a beautiful type of the eternal union between Christ and the Church which is His Body, His Bride (Ephesians 5:25). Just as God saw Eve in Adam, He saw us in Christ before the foundation of the world. We are told that God caused a deep sleep to fall upon Adam, and one of his ribs "builded He into a woman" (Revised Version Margin, Genesis 2:22) which He brought to him.

The second man was to go through the deep sleep of the death of the cross in order that He might have a Bride to present to Himself one day (Ephesians 5:27). Adam's bride was literally a member of his body, and we who form Christ's Bride are members of His body (Ephesians 5:30), the church which He is currently building comprising all believers (Matthew 16:18). The supreme purpose of God's overall plan in creation is seen to be the obtaining of a bride for His Son, "the fulness of Him that fills all in all" (Ephesians 1:23).

Blest be the wisdom and the power

The Justice and the Grace,

That joined in council to restore

And save our ruined race.

Our father ate forbidden fruit,

And from his glory fell,

And we his children thus were brought

To death and near to hell.

Blest be the Lord who sent His Son,

To take our flesh and blood,

To bring us life He gave His own

And made our peace with God.

He honoured all His Father's laws

Which we have disobeyed;

He bore our sins upon the cross

And our full ransom paid.

(Isaac Watts)

# CHAPTER TWENTY-ONE: THE APOSTLE (BRIAN JOHNSTON)

The exhortation to consider Jesus as the Apostle was originally given to Jewish Christians who were in spiritual danger. They needed to be warned not to drift, fall or be carried away. What was the problem? They were leaning back toward the Law, and, in the process, their hearts were becoming hardened. In warning, the writer recalls to them the provocation Israel caused God by its hardening of heart on account of the lack of water at Rephidim (Exodus 17:1). In that regard we read specifically of the temptation (Hebrews 3:8). Israel put God to the test by asking in particular: "Is the LORD among us, or not?" Instead of trusting God for help in adverse circumstances, they demanded a miracle to reveal His Presence.

Both in the letter to the Hebrews (Hebrews 3:7) and in Psalm 95 (verse 7) which was being cited, we find the expression "His voice". The Old Testament is referring to Jehovah's voice; while in Hebrews it is in the context of God speaking in His Son. How unmistakably the Spirit of God underlines for us the fact that Jehovah the Lord of the Old Testament is Jesus the Apostle and Messiah of the New Testament, the One through whom God has spoken to us, and whom these Jews were to consider.

The word "consider" as found in the Revised Version carries the force of "to consider attentively" or, as the New International Version renders it, "to fix your thoughts on". This again brings us to the danger these people were in. They had been allowing their attention to wander, so that their gaze was slowly turning back to the Law. To deliver themselves they must set their minds on Jesus, firstly as the Apostle. The term "apostle" conveys the idea of sending someone off on a commission to do something, having furnished him with credentials. In the Greek version of the Old Testament, the verb from the same word is used of God sending Moses. In this letter the writer, by the Spirit, compares the two apostles of the eras of the Law and Grace.

Viewed as the Apostle, Jesus is the One who came out from the presence of God in order to bring God's Word to us. Previously, the prophets had brought God's Word to His people, but in the first chapter of Hebrews we are caused to consider Jesus the Apostle as the heir of all things, as the Creator of the worlds, as the brightness of eternal glory, as the expression of the divine essence, as the sustainer of the universe, and as the sacrifice that purges (a people) from sin.

In these ways, the superiority of Jesus as the Apostle is set before us. We contrast, in passing, the fading, reflected glory that radiated from the face of Moses the apostle of the Law, as compared with the unfading, inherent, surpassing glory possessed by our Apostle. God has spoken to us. The eternal Son, from Godhead's fullest glory, was the One whom the Father sanctified and sent into the world to bring us His Word. God had formerly spoken to His Old Testament people at the time of their constitution, when, from a mountain burning with fire to the heart of heaven, He had thundered the Decalogue, the Ten Commandments. That was, we are told, a "word spoken through angels", and so it was not to be regarded lightly.

Israel, alas, discovered to their cost that every disobedience received a just recompense. This showed that God's Word through these "sent ones" proved steadfast. In our case, the Sent One (Apostle) is Jesus, and chapter one of Hebrews argues that He is "by so much better than the angels". Jesus' supremacy is established by virtue of His unique Sonship relation to God the Father, the fact that angels are instructed to worship Him, the special way in which He is addressed as God by God, the fact that He is the Creator, and because He has been exalted in His victory to the highest place.

Now, since God's Word has been brought to us by Jesus, the Apostle of our confession, One who is demonstrably so much better than the angels, "therefore" (Hebrews 2:1) we really ought to pay even more attention to that Word, bearing in mind that that which had been spoken through angels had proved steadfast. Indeed, we must be more careful than Israel not to neglect our salvation. This is a warning that a people needs to hear.

The letter to the Hebrews envisages a divinely gathered people on earth engaged in the collective service of God. Remembering how Israel had been saved out of Egypt by blood, passed through the "baptism" of their Red Sea experience and then pledged their obedience to God's Word while arranged around Mount Sinai, we judge that this appeal from the heart of God has in view the anti-type of Israel's Sinai experience.

Jesus is described as the Apostle of our "confession". The full force of this word could be expressed as "to speak the same thing as another", or "to agree with someone else". When, at Sinai, Moses, God's apostle to His people then, brought the Word to them, their confession on that occasion was: "all that the LORD has spoken will we do, and be obedient" (Exodus 24:7). If today we find ourselves in a church of God, among the people of God, keeping the Word of God brought to us by Jesus the Apostle, then we have made the same confession, or should have. The thing that legitimizes a claim to be the people of God is this "good confession", or agreement to keep, in its entirety, the Word of God as delivered by the Apostle, and now written down for us by the apostles and prophets in the New Testament of our Bibles.

Some people find that they cannot agree with certain things in the New Testament. They appropriate to themselves the liberty to be selective in their obedience. That sort of attitude has' no place among the people of God. God has spoken, and the people of God are to "speak the same thing" Our confession means agreeing with God even, alas, if it means disagreeing with other dear children of God.

Should we get discouraged, like Israel, perhaps by smallness locally or by lack of results, let us not be found putting God to the test by questioning "Is the LORD among us, or not?" May we rather take as a timely word the encouragement to refocus our eyes on the Apostle of our confession, even Jesus. If we find ourselves in danger of "coming short" or "shrinking back" or not holding fast our boldness, let us look to Jesus. He is worthy of our undivided attention, since He is proclaimed here to be greater than the prophets, the angels and Moses.

Sent from th'eternal Father

Who dwells in light above

Came forth the Son most holy

To manifest His love.

Then glory to the Father

For us, His Son He gave

To Christ, Kinsman-Redeemer,

He died our souls to save.

(C.M. Luxmoore)

# CHAPTER TWENTY-TWO: THE WORD (BRIAN JOHNSTON)

When the apostle John, by the Spirit, used the title 'Word' (Greek: Logos) he was using a term familiar to the Greek mind of his day. The Greeks used it to express the principle, or rationale, which they understood to be behind the creation of the universe. What came as a revelation from God through John's writing was the identification of this abstract creation principle with a person, God the Son. That this is a title of the Lord Jesus is quite clear from verse 14 of John chapter 1: 'The Word became flesh'. God the Son became flesh in order to reveal the eternal God to us.

With that in mind, we might still ask ourselves: 'Why this particular title?' We think of how we ourselves use words in order to communicate with each other. We reveal what's in our mind by our words. The eternal God has expressed his mind in the one who is the Word. In Jesus, the Word, God has fully revealed his character and perfectly declared his will. What can we learn about God's Son from the opening verses of John's Gospel, where he's introduced to us as the Word? What sort of person is he? Seven points have been noted (by J.I. Packer).

1. He was 'in the beginning' (v.1). This reminds us of the opening words of the Bible, which take us back to the time of the creation. In other words, the first thing we learn here about the Word is his pre-existence. He didn't 'become', nor was he 'made', as is said of other things in the following verses. What this shows is his eternity, and it's confirmed by so many other Bible texts. 'He is before all (created) things', according to Colossians 1:17. This echoes the prophecy of Micah that the one who was to be born in Bethlehem - the Word become flesh - would be

one whose 'goings forth are from of old, from everlasting' (Micah 5:2). Yes, the Word is the eternal Word.

2. He was 'with God' (v.1, literally 'towards God'). The word (Greek: pros) translated here as 'with' conveys the idea of communion between distinct persons. It indicates personal companionship and the enjoyment of fellowship together. This teaches us about the personality of the Word, as someone capable of complete fellowship with God the Father and the Holy Spirit. In other words, the Word is the personal Word.

3. He 'was God' (v.1). That's really plain, but this statement has been made the centre of controversy by false teachers. We may be absolutely clear that to insert the indefinite article (an 'a' – as in 'he was a god') is completely wrong grammatically. There's no question on which side the qualified experts are, as witness the rules of Greek grammar that even a novice can read – and find this very example discussed. Therefore, as it stands, it gives crystal clear testimony to the deity of the Word. In any case, this truth is very clear from many other Bible texts; two from Matthew will serve as our examples. In Matthew 3:1-6, we see how John the Baptist fulfils the prophecy of Isaiah 40:3 – which talked about preparing the way for the Lord, and the Baptist relates that to his very own work preparing the way for the Lord Jesus, which means Jesus is the very one whom Isaiah called God. Matthew then takes up another of Isaiah's great prophecies in describing the birth of the Lord Jesus in terms of Isaiah's predicting of the virgin-born Immanuel (Isaiah 1:22-23), whose name means 'God with us.'

Many among the cults profess difficulty with the truth of the Trinity. And while it's absolutely true that the term 'trinity' isn't found in the Bible, its truth certainly is. As Luke records the announcement to Mary by Gabriel concerning the birth of the Lord, we've clear reference made to the deity of the one who is to be born, and to the fact of the trinity.

# SPARKLING FACETS: BIBLE NAMES AND TITLES OF JESUS

In the first chapter of Luke, the child to be born is declared to be 'the Son of the Most High' or the 'Son of God'. It's prophesied that the conception would be a work of the 'Holy Spirit' (v.35) and that the 'Lord God' would give the child the throne of David (v.32).

There are references to three distinct persons there at one moment in time as we view it, and all with the same nature, existing as one God. In the first chapter of John's Gospel, John the Baptist publicly witnesses to the Lord Jesus as being the Lamb of God (v.29) and the Son of God (v.34); so the Lord is presented in that first chapter as the Word, the Lamb, and the Son. This Word is without doubt the divine Word.

4. 'All things were made by Him' (v.3). Here we find the Word creating. Paul begins his letter to the Colossians with the same truth: 'For in Him were all things created…all things have been created through Him, and unto Him' (Colossians 1:16). Nothing could be clearer than this, and it must be our final answer to the atheistic evolutionist.

5. 'In Him was life' (v.4). And now we find the Word animating. He's the source of all life, whether natural or spiritual. Paul's words to the Athenians (Acts 17:25,28) certainly apply to him: 'He Himself gives to all life', and 'in Him we live'. Whereas, regarding spiritual life: 'this life is in His Son' (1 John 5:11).

6. 'And the life was the light of men' (v.4). That is, here's the Word now revealing and enlightening. He's the true light that lights everyone (v.9). All, without excuse, should have a certain consciousness of God.

7. 'And the Word became flesh' (v.14). This is the truth of the incarnation, of how this eternal, personal, divine Word, the Creator, Animator and Revealer of all, came into his creation.

In Philippians, Paul writes of the Lord emptying himself and 'being made in the likeness of men' (Philippians 2:7). We read with wonder from Genesis 1:26 how God said, 'Let us make man in Our image, after

Our likeness'; yet here we have the infinitely greater miracle of one who is God but now in man's likeness. In eternity, as the Son of God, he emptied himself; in time, as the Son of Man, he humbled himself. The giving of himself was something that began in eternity, before he even came to earth to be born.

There are two points that we need to be clear about. First, that it wasn't of his deity that the Lord emptied himself in becoming flesh. We've already made reference to the fact that he was 'God with us', and the Bible repeatedly declares that the one whom the Father sent into the world was 'the Son' (e.g. 1 John 4:14). He was 'the Son' before, and after, his birth at Bethlehem.

Secondly, we must affirm that he became truly human. The Gospels faithfully record for us the reality of his humanity in describing his tiredness and thirst. Only as someone who was truly man could he suffer and bleed and die in our place as the sacrifice for our sins. These twin truths of his deity and of his humanity are both to be found in John 1:14: 'And the Word became flesh, and dwelt among us and we beheld His glory, glory as of the only begotten from the Father, full of grace and truth.' Thus, the tiny infant form that was upheld in the arms of Mary his mother, was at the same time the Mighty God simultaneously 'upholding all things by the word of His power' (Hebrews 1:3). Well might we say in the words of the Bible: "Without controversy great is the mystery of godliness; He who was manifested in the flesh"! (1 Timothy 3:16).

As well as John 1, there are two other places in the New Testament where the Lord is presented as the Word. They are: 1 John 1, and then also in Revelation 19:11-16 which views the Word as the Judge. How different his return to earth will be from his first Advent! For he will come at the head of the armies of heaven to wage the fearful campaign of Armageddon and to judge the nations still alive at that time.

# SPARKLING FACETS: BIBLE NAMES AND TITLES OF JESUS

The letter to the Hebrews opens by informing us that God has spoken in his Son (the Word whom we've been tracing). This not only means through the teaching of Jesus of Nazareth but also and especially through his person and his actions, for in these the glory of God was seen. In Hebrews 1:2-4, he's given the highest imaginable descriptive titles both in relation to the universe – for he's called Creator, Upholder, Heir - and also in relation to God himself – when he's also called the radiance, the image, and the Son. This glorious and unique person is presented as the grand finale, or last word, of God's self-disclosure. With Peter, who was an eyewitness of his majesty on the mountain of Transfiguration, we might also say 'such a voice' (2 Peter 1:17)!

And yet the Word was never more awesome than when he answered nothing to his accusers. The Silent Logos (or Word)! The silence of the Word then expressed as perfectly as ever the glory of the eternal God.

# CHAPTER TWENTY-THREE: THE MEDIATOR AND THE ADVOCATE (J. McCORMICK)

In 1 Timothy 2, the mediating work of Christ is brought before us as a central and fundamental truth, based on which exhortations to those in the house of God are given: "that supplications, prayers, intercessions and giving of thanks, be made for all men"; "This is good and acceptable in the sight of God our Saviour; who desires all men to be saved, and come to the knowledge of the truth. For there is one God and one Mediator also between God and men, the Man, Christ Jesus, who gave Himself a Ransom for all, to be testified in due time."

The three-time repetition of the word "all" in these verses is interesting. The range of our prayers, and the extent of testimony is universal, for, and toward all men. The salvation of all men comes within the ambit of God's will, and this is proved by the fact that Christ gave Himself a Ransom for all. The mediating work of Christ is therefore seen to be, between God and all men. A mediator is one who comes between two parties for a definite purpose. If the parties are estranged or in dispute, a mediator may cause reconciliation and bring about agreement. If the purpose is to find common ground of agreement with a view to future relationships being established, a mediator may act in stating or conveying the terms and conditions necessary to both parties coming into covenant relationship. Both of these purposes are seen in Scripture.

Moses stands out conspicuously as mediator in the deliverance of the children of Israel from the slavery of Egypt. He acted on God's behalf in dealing with the proud and mighty Pharaoh, and on behalf of the children of Israel in their trouble and sorrow. He is also seen as the mediator of the covenant between God and Israel after their miraculous deliverance from Egypt. When they came to Sinai, God gave them His law, "it was ordained through angels by the hand of a mediator" (Galatians 3:19).

Moses later said, "I stood between the LORD and you at that time, to declare to you the word of the LORD" (Deuteronomy 5:5). "And Moses ... laid before them all these words which the LORD commanded him." "And Moses brought back the words of the people to the LORD" (Exodus 19:6, 8). So, upon the acceptance of the conditions laid down by God in His law, they became His people, and He became their God in covenant relationship, and the covenant was dedicated with blood, sprinkled upon the altar, the book and all the people.

The mediating of Christ excels that of Moses, even as the new covenant has an abiding, surpassing glory, excelling that which passes away (2 Corinthians 3:11). In this dispensation - of grace all national distinctions have been obliterated in the great mediating work of the cross. All men are seen to be accountable to one God. The whole of the human race is under sin, under the authority of darkness, without hope and without God in the world, and brought under the judgement of God. If deliverance is to be achieved for men, it must be by a man who can stand between God and men to represent both, and effect reconciliation. Such a man could never be found in Adam's fallen race. "Nor is there any mediator between us, who may lay his hand on us both" said Job (Job 9:33).

Jesus is the One who came down out of heaven, the Son of Man among the sons of men - perfect, spotless, sinless, holy, harmless, undefiled. Only he could be the Mediator between God and men in the question of sin, which had estranged men from God. God could only meet men in judgement, unless someone could stand between to bear that judgement, and satisfy the claims of divine righteousness. Christ became answerable for the whole of the human race. Of His own freewill He gave Himself a Ransom for all, and this has been accepted. There is, and can be, only one Mediator between God and men, the claims and pretensions of mere sinful men, whoever they are, are nullified by this clear statement of fact: "There is one Mediator."

In His mediating work, Jesus did not act as a neutral on behalf of other parties, as though He had no personal interest. He stood between God and men with an intense personal interest in both, and He acted according to the necessities of the case in the interests of both.

We may think of the Godward side of that work in which He revealed, as the Mediator, the infinite pity, love, grace, and mercy of God to men. "Then He is gracious to him, and says, Deliver him from going down to the pit, I have found a Ransom" (Job 33:24).

He would not, and could not, misrepresent God in the slightest degree, He could not by-pass the least of God's claims - God's honour must be upheld and vindicated in full and absolute righteousness. At the cross He was actively engaged in this work because He willed to act, for He Himself had a real personal interest in the outcome, as He acted as Mediator between God and men. On the other hand, He representatively acted on behalf of all men in becoming accountable Himself. The life of perfect obedience which men could not live, because of sin, was lived by Him. As the only perfect Man who had fulfilled the requirements of the law, He yielded His life substitutionally in sacrifice, a Ransom for all.

So, in His mediating work, He acted on behalf of men in rendering full satisfaction to God by His obedience unto death. He identified Himself with the race of men (sin apart) and by His work procured the fullest blessings it was possible for divine favour to bestow. In this too He had a real personal interest - He did not stand detached, for He Himself is "Man, Christ Jesus." Eternity will reveal the full results of

His mighty mediating work eternity, but we know now, that "... when we were enemies, we were reconciled to God through the death of His Son" (Romans 5:10).

"He is the Mediator of a better covenant, which was established on better promises" (Hebrews 8:6). Unconditional blessings flow out to the believer in Christ on the basis of what He has done once for all, "having been once offered." "For by one offering He has perfected forever those that are being sanctified" and "Their sins and their lawless deeds I will remember no more" (Hebrews 10:14, 17). "He is the Mediator," not was. He abides, and His work abides, and so He is Himself the Guarantor of all the promised blessings of the covenant. There are also conditional blessings of the new covenant for those upon whose hearts and minds the Spirit of God has written God's law and who respond to it in obedience (Hebrews 8:10; 10:16).

## The Advocate

The only place where the word "advocate" is used in relation to Jesus is in 1 John 2:1. The same word is used four times in reference to the Holy Spirit, and is translated "Comforter" (John 14:16; John 14:26; John 15:26; John 16:7) in the Revised Version. It means one called alongside of another to help, counsel, comfort, befriend, to take his part, to represent, and plead his cause. It is evident from John 14.16 that the Lord Jesus was, while on earth, the true Comforter of His disciples, for He says, "And I will pray the Father, and He shall give you another Comforter, that He may be with you for ever (RV)".

The Lord Jesus has died, and has been raised from the dead. No longer now on earth, He is an Advocate with the Father. That other Comforter, the Holy Spirit, has been sent, and indwells every believer; hence we have two Comforters or Advocates, the Holy Spirit present with us, and Jesus Christ the righteous in God's presence for us.

It is for our encouragement, as we journey on through this wilderness toward His Father's house, to that place that Christ is preparing for us, that we have the present help, counsel, guidance and comfort of the Holy Spirit. True comfort has the thought of helping and strengthening, as well as consoling, and we need all of this in this dark, cold world; "The Spirit Himself makes intercession for us with groanings which cannot be uttered" (Romans 8:26). As we journey on through the temptations of sin, beset by the snares of the devil, and the evil tendencies of the flesh within, it is evident that God has graciously foreseen and provided for the needs of His children as they may stumble and fall, and perhaps be overcome by sin.

There is no such thing in this world as sinless perfection, for "If we say that we have not sinned, we make Him a liar, and His word is not in us" (1 John 1:10). Nevertheless. there is nevertheless no licence given in Scripture for sinning. "My little children, these things write I to you, so that you may not sin" (1 John 2:1). "Shall we continue in sin, that grace may abound? Certainly not! How shall we who died to sin live any longer in it?" (Romans 6:1,2).

Sin today is being made to look respectable by medical or psychological terms. The public conscience is being hardened. Lying, stealing, and all kinds of deceit is practised, and is considered of little account; just the thing to do if you can get away with it, seems to be the general attitude.

It would be extremely sad if children of God were affected by these standards of conduct - the believer is called upon to "put to death the deeds of the body" by the Spirit, and he "will live" (see Romans 8:12-14). We can't, however, prevent the presence of sin in us. The old man, that evil and corrupt nature within, is always active, seeking to use our members in sin's service, that it might occupy the throne of our hearts. Hence the injunction: "Therefore do not let sin reign in your mortal body, that you should obey it in its lusts." (Romans 6:11).

After using all the resources at our disposal to prevent us from sinning, which we should, we are nevertheless conscious every day of the defiling power of sin affecting our thoughts, words and deeds, and we might well be downcast and despairing if we had no Advocate. "And if anyone sins, we have an Advocate with the Father, Jesus Christ the righteous" (1 John 2:1). We have an Advocate, and He is the propitiation for our sins.

Everything that Christ has done in relation to sin finds its true value in Himself, and "with" (toward) the Father, as our Advocate, is the righteous One. Being righteous in His own Person, and in all He has done, and is doing, He will never plead an unrighteous cause before a righteous Father. He is Himself the answer to every accusation, and His advocacy on behalf of God's children is effectual because of His intrinsic righteousness.

Let us not treat sin lightly, for what sin means to God can only (to a degree) be understood by us in the light of the dreadful sufferings of the Cross. God longs that His children will keep in fellowship with Him, hence, "If we confess our sins," the advocacy of Christ, and the all-sufficiency of His precious blood, provide a perfect reason for the exercise of forgiveness, and so "He is faithful and just to forgive us our sins, and to cleanse us from all unrighteousness" (1 John 1:9).

In heaven before God's holy face,

Behold an Advocate

Who intercedes for us in grace,

With power divinely great.

He loves us deeply, this we know

By tokens that he wears;

Pierced hands and feet and side, all show

The matchless love he bears.

He died to ransom us from sin,

He lives to save us still

From every power without, within

That seeks to work us ill.

He, touched with trials that attend

The weakness of our frame

Can sympathetic succour lend,

For He has known the same.

He overcame His mightiest foe,

When He earth's pathway trod;

And victory we may also know,

Who come through Him to God.

Fear not to come, if sin o'ertake,

Confessing all to God,

Who will forgive us for His sake,

And cleanse us by His blood.

Christ will fresh strength for conflict give

The needed grace impart,

That each below for Him may live,

And He live in each heart.

(C. Belton)

# CHAPTER TWENTY-FOUR: MY BELOVED (ANON)

---

The expression, "My Beloved," which occurs so frequently in the Song of Songs, is also one of the special names of the Lord Jesus Christ, whom God describes as "My Beloved in whom My soul is well pleased" (Matthew 12:18), and tells us what He is to God, His Father. In chapter 5 of the Song of Songs there are some very beautiful words, poetically descriptive of one called "My Beloved," and in this poetic imagery we may see illustrations of certain truths relative to our Lord Jesus, truths which are abundantly evidenced elsewhere in Scripture - some of the wonders of that Blessed One who is described as "altogether lovely."

"What is your beloved more than another beloved?" is the question asked by the daughters of Jerusalem. This question receives an answer that gives a most wonderful portrayal of the deeply imprinted image of an absent one. If we can speak of our Beloved as she did of her beloved we shall do well.

**"My beloved is white and ruddy"**

Two truths are expressed here which must stand at the forefront of our witness for the Lord Jesus. White is a symbol of purity, and the purity of the Lord Jesus is beyond all that earth can produce and is of heavenly origin. This is shown in Matthew 17:2 when He was on the mountain "and His face did shine as the sun, and His garments became white as the light," as the divine radiance from His glorious Person shone through and transformed them, making them "glistering, exceeding white, so as no fuller on earth can whiten them" (Mark 9:3). Ruddy signifies healthy humanity, and is used to describe David at the time of his anointing by Samuel. It reminds us of Him who took the form of a Servant and was found in fashion as a Man, sharing in blood and flesh.

**"The Chiefest among ten thousand"**

This suggests One who is pre-eminent, unique and peerless.

"Man so perfect!

Holy, noble, humble too."

Ten thousand of the greatest names blazoned on the pages of history beside His, fade from view as the stars when the sun arises. He has no peer!

**"His head is as the most fine gold"**

Here is the truth of headship, so plainly taught in Scripture, but so little thought of today. Gold is symbolic in Scripture of that which is of God, divine in origin. So a church of God is spoken of as a golden lampstand (Revelation 1:20). Daniel, in his interpretation of King Nebuchadnezzar's dream of the image with a head of gold, said, "The God of heaven has given you a kingdom ... you are this head of gold" (Daniel 2:37, 38). The headship of Christ is illustrated by the words "Most fine gold," signifying headship in its highest form. Thus our Beloved is "Head over all things to the Church which is His Body" and He has all authority in heaven and on earth, for His God has put "all things in subjection under His feet" (1 Corinthians 15:27). Let us learn this much needed truth for today - subjection of heart and life to Him whose bond-servants we should be.

**"His locks are bushy and black as a raven"**

If, as has been suggested, His divine authority is seen in the head of most fine gold, so His glorious Manhood is seen in the locks. "Bushy" and "black" - each contains precious thoughts of our Lord Jesus. With humanity age is marked by the thinning or greying of the hair, but of Him it is said His locks are bushy and black. In Hosea 7:9 it is said of Ephraim, "strangers have devoured his strength ... yea, grey hairs are here and there upon him," but our Beloved, our glorious Head, is alive in the power of an endless life. There is no diminishing of strength with Him for it is written:

> "You, Lord, in the beginning laid the foundation of the earth, and the heavens are the work of Your hands. They will perish, but You remain; And they will all grow old like a garment; Like a cloak You will fold them up, and they will be changed. But You are the same, and Your years will not fail" (Hebrews 1:10-12).

**"His eyes are like doves beside the water brooks"**

The eyes are the most expressive members of the face. In them, the inward emotion can often be easily read. Love, anger, fear, pity and reproach all can be expressed through the eyes. John describes the eyes of the Lord as being like a flame of fire (Revelation 1:14). Here the Lord is presented as the all-seeing One, who repeats to each church the words "I know", though what He knew of each church was different. But, in this Song, love is the distinctive characteristic.

Gentleness and tender feeling,

Pity too, and grace

Softly lustred all Thy dealing

With our stricken race

Thou with sympathy and healing

Mid our woes didst move,

Every gracious deed revealing

Thou, O Lord, art love. (C. Belton)

The unjust, blasphemous reproaches of His enemies broke the heart of the Lord Jesus (Psalm 69:20). But the look of love, mingled perhaps with grief, broke Peter's heart after his denial, for "he went out and wept bitterly." The bride here recalls only the tender love of those eyes. We too, in a spiritual sense, can realize that look of love.

As the Lord Jesus moved about on this earth His eyes were always on the look-out for some good to do. How frequently we read that as He passed by "He saw"! It may have been a man or a woman in need of Him, the blind, the lepers, a weeping widow or a multitude in distress, but the response always was the same: "He was moved with compassion." One day we shall meet Him; "How shall I meet those eyes? Those eyes once looked down from the Cross, searching the faces of those around, fulfilling the words of Psalm 69:20, "And I looked for some to take pity, but there was none and for comforters, but I found none." But when we see Him it will be in His radiant glory, anointed with the oil of gladness, in the fulness of the joy of His Father's presence.

### "His cheeks are as a bed of spices, as banks of sweet herbs"

Yet most shamefully and ruthlessly did His enemies pluck the hair from that lovely face when He gave His back to the smiters, and His cheeks to them that plucked off the hair, when He hid not His face from shame and spitting (Isaiah 50:6). In some respects, this was the most shameful thing they did to Him. In the days of the law, if a man refused to do the kinsman's part (see Deuteronomy 25:5-10), the aggrieved widow would "spit in his face" and he stood shamed forever. What a contrast with the One who had left the eternal throne and was born of a woman for the express purpose of becoming the Kinsman-Redeemer!

To be spit upon! Surely, surely, the shame all belongs to those who so acted.

**"His lips are as lilies, dropping liquid myrrh"**

This would speak to us of the words of Him of whom, at the beginning of His public ministry it is written: "And all bore witness to Him witness and marvelled at the gracious words of grace which came out of His mouth" (Luke 4:22). What wonderful words He spoke! Words His Father had given Him to speak. He Himself knew every scripture which told of His sufferings and death. Thus to the two disciples on the Emmaus road He said, "Ought not the Christ to have suffered these things? ... And beginning at Moses and all the prophets, He expounded to them in all the Scriptures the things concerning Himself." What liquid myrrh was here! The very quintessence of Scripture witnessing to the sufferings of the Christ.

**"His hands are as rings of gold set with beryl"**

The hands speak of action. "Your hands have made me and fashioned me." "The heavens are the work of Your hands." "The work of Your fingers, the moon and the stars, which You have ordained." These Scriptures confirm the thought that the hands speak of the actions of the One "who went about doing good." How wonderful was the grace of Him who touched the leper with cleansing power, who touched the blind eyes to give sight, who touched the bier on which the dead son of a widow lay, who took the daughter of Jairus by the hand, and raised her up!

The rings, being of gold, remind us that all His actions were according to the will of His Father, as He said: "I do always the things that are pleasing to Him." It can be truly said of Him what could be said of no other: "No word ever needed to be recalled, no action regretted, no step retraced." All was perfect.

All His life was right

And holy in God's sight:

The Son of God so true

No sin He ever knew,

Those kind hands that did much good,

They nailed them to a cross of wood.

**"His body is as ivory work, overlaid with sapphires"**

Of His body it is written, "a body You have prepared for Me" (Hebrews 10:5). He had a human mother, but no human father. He had a body like ours, yet having no inherent sin, a body in which He glorified God on the earth and accomplished the work He had given Him to do; a body which was laid at last in the tomb, but which saw no corruption, indeed could not see corruption. Ivory fittingly speaks of this. It's a happy thought that "we have been sanctified through the offering of the body of Jesus Christ once for all" (Hebrews 10:10).

**"His legs are as pillars of marble"**

Here strength is clearly intended. While it is true that "the LORD has no pleasure in the legs of a man," yet it is equally true that He found infinite pleasure in the strength of will and purpose always seen in Him who never wavered, but set His face like a flint to go to Jerusalem. We read of one of the days, just prior to His going to the Cross, these words: "Jesus was going before them; and they were amazed" (Mark 10:32). Doubtless the unflinching determination and unfaltering step of that lonely, majestic Figure, as "He went on before" (Luke 19:24), was something the like of which they had never seen. "Marching in the greatness of His strength," is a word which awaits fulfilment, yet here is something akin to it. He stands out in grand and glorious contrast to all who have ever walked this earth.

Oh Christ, He is the fountain,

The deep, sweet well of love

The streams on earth I've tasted,

More deep I'll drink above.

There to an ocean fullness

His mercy doth expand,

And glory, glory dwelleth

In Immanuel's land!

Oh, I am my Beloved's

And my Beloved's mine!

He brings a poor vile sinner

Into His house of wine,

I stand upon His merit

I know no safer stand,

Not e'en where glory dwelleth,

In Immanuel's land.

The Bride eyes not her garment

But her dear Bridegroom's face

I will not gaze at glory

But on my King of grace.

Not at the crown He giveth,

But on his pierced hand;

The Lamb is all the glory

Of Immanuel's land.

(A.R. Cousin)

# CHAPTER TWENTY-FIVE: THE SHEPHERD (T.W. FULLARTON)

One of the precious titles of Jesus used to illustrate the relationship between the Lord Jesus and those on earth that He calls His own is that of the Shepherd. The same illustration is used frequently throughout the Old Testament concerning Jehovah and His people, Israel: "He will feed His flock like a shepherd, He will gather the lambs with His arm, and carry them in His bosom, and gently lead those that give who are with young" (Isaiah 40:11). It is also written, "Give ear, O Shepherd of Israel, You who lead Joseph like a flock" (Psalm 80:1).

Who of God's children hasn't read or memorized and often found comfort from the record of the experience of David in Psalm 23? David could look back over a life of both sweet and bitter experiences; with its contrast of green pastures and still waters and the valley of the shadow of death, and with the confidence born of personal experience could say, "Jehovah is my Shepherd."

If Israel as His flock, and individuals as His sheep, could know the shepherd-care of Jehovah-Rohi, whom we judge to be also the Good, Great and Chief Shepherd of the New Testament, how much more should we, who "were going astray like sheep" (1 Peter 2:25), know and experience the shepherd-care of our Lord Jesus Christ, who once as the Good Shepherd gave His life for the sheep, and now in resurrection life lives as the Great Shepherd to feed, guide, comfort and protect His own and as the Chief Shepherd is coming again!

**The Good Shepherd**

In John 10, the Lord Jesus speaks of this relationship which He bears to His sheep. He who had been a Shepherd to Israel, that flock which He had once led by the hand of Moses and Aaron (Psalm 77:20) and later, by the skilful hands of David (Psalm 78:72), now looked out with a sad heart upon that flock scattered far and wide - wayward sheep which had strayed from the green pastures into which He'd led them, and from under His protecting rod.

The foolish under-shepherds of a later day had led them astray and neglected their charge, until they had become meat for all the beasts of the field (Ezekiel 34:1-10). Now, in His gracious dealings with the children of men, He longs to experience again that relationship with those He desires to call His own. But to establish this relationship certain steps must be taken. He must win the heart and confidence of those He would lead. They must get to know Him and to realize that He cares for them, and that His thoughts towards them are only good.

So, to gain their confidence, the initial steps are taken; downward from the throne of heaven (from which He had been the Shepherd of Israel) He came to dwell among men as a Sharer of blood and flesh. But the sheep He had now come to gather, were lost, whether of Israel or the Gentiles, and so He must first seek and save that which was lost. In the parable of Luke 15:3-7 the shepherd is seen going after the lost sheep "until he find it"; a seeking that involved discomfort, hardship and risk. But when we turn to the reality in John 10, we see the life of the Good Shepherd "laid down" for the sheep; nothing less was needed to rescue the lost ones.

Surely when we ponder over this and realize what He has done our heart and confidence have been gained! As the hymnwriter has said:

Our Lord His glory laid aside,

That He had known with God.

Then came to earth as Man and died

To cleanse us by His blood.

Good Shepherd He stray sheep He sought,

Stooped low and suffered loss;

He bore the hiding of God's face,

A curse upon the cross.

John the Baptist, as a true under-shepherd, had succeeded by his message in gathering some of the lost and perplexed ones of Israel's scattered flock, but in the purpose of God this gathering was to lead to incorporation in the objective of the death of Jesus – "One flock; one Shepherd." The Baptist's ministry was exclusively to Israel, but the Lord Jesus had others in view, as He said, "Other sheep I have, which are not of this fold: them also I must bring, and they shall hear My voice; and they shall become one flock, one Shepherd" (John 10:16).

**The Great Shepherd**

The life He laid down was confirmation of the fact that He would hold nothing back in order that the purpose of God might be accomplished, "that He might ... gather together into one the children of God that are scattered abroad" (John 11:52). From a human standpoint, it would have appeared at His death that such a purpose had been defeated, for the Shepherd had been smitten and the sheep of the flock had been scattered (Matthew 26:31). Where now was the possibility of there being "one flock, one Shepherd"? But these questions, about which neither men nor angels yet knew anything, were judicially settled at Calvary.

The climax to these days of bewilderment and doubt was reached when "the God of peace," who had found perfect and complete satisfaction in Christ's atoning death, "brought again from the dead the Great Shepherd of the sheep in the blood of the eternal covenant" (Hebrews 13:20). The greatness of the good Shepherd was now being displayed. The most terrible of all the foes of the little flock had been met and defeated, and Satan, death, the grave and Sheol had now lost their power and terrors. No longer could the fear of death and that which lay beyond it keep those who were Christ's in bondage (Hebrews 2:14, 15). They would be free to "serve Him without fear" (Luke 1:74).

And now, their hands having handled Him, their eyes having beheld Him, first in life before the cross, then in resurrection, all doubts have been dispelled about His goodness and greatness. He is raised to the right hand of the throne of the Majesty in the heavens and, as the Great Shepherd and the Chief Shepherd, He shepherds His heavenly people in a world where they are "strangers and pilgrims" (1 Peter 2:11). Such are spoken of as having been like sheep going astray, "but are now returned unto the Shepherd" of their souls (verse 25). He who had stood between them and the foe and is now on the throne, having had all authority given unto Him, as the Great Shepherd still cares for, protects and delivers His sheep.

"He's risen now, and lives on high,

Again He's glorified,

And ever liveth there to save

His sheep for whom He died.

As Shepherd Great, with crook in hand,

He tends them all with care,

E'en through death's shadow, and midst foes,

He's present with them there."

Well may we sing:

"Jesus is our Shepherd

Guarded by His arm,

Though the wolves may ravin

None can do us harm:

Should we tread death's valley

Dark with fearful gloom

We will fear no evil

Victors o'er the tomb."

## The Chief Shepherd

The result of the Lord's resurrection and the joy and confidence that brought was to bring together again the "little flock," now prepared to follow where the Shepherd might lead. During the forty days following His resurrection, He truly led His own, making them to lie down in green pastures and leading them beside the still waters. But He cannot remain with them, and those whom He had chosen must go out to seek the lost with the divine message of love and mercy and grace. In those forty days words of the All-wise One were "given from one Shepherd" (Ecclesiastes 12:11), unfolding the Old Testament Scriptures which spoke of Him, whereby the hearts of His disciples were caused to burn within them, as in Luke 24:32.

But there was now a New Covenant of grace, and things related to it, which they must know in order that the under-shepherds might be fitted to gather and feed the Flock of God (1 Peter 5:2; Acts 20:28). Following His ascension and glorification and the descent of the Holy

Spirit, preachers go out, equipped with the divine message and the power of the Holy Spirit. Those who hear and believe the message are taught how the Great Shepherd would lead them according to the Scriptures, and with hearts bowed in simple and humble dependence upon Him they follow Him. So we read: "They then that received his word were baptized: and there were added unto them in that day about three thousand souls. And they continued stedfastly in the apostles' teaching and fellowship, in the breaking of bread and the prayers" (Acts 2:41,42).

They did not become many flocks, but one flock only under one Shepherd. In the many churches of God, the under-shepherds are all responsible to the Chief Shepherd to tend and feed the Flock, each one in his allotted portion.

The New Testament Scriptures speak very preciously of the Lord Jesus in His threefold character as Shepherd. How much do we each know of Him as that? All who know Him as their Saviour have experienced something of His care as the Good Shepherd and the Great Shepherd. As the Chief Shepherd, He still calls on those who hear and know His voice to follow wherever He leads. How and where does He lead? This much we now say, He leads by His Spirit through the Scriptures and He guides into the "one flock" expressed in churches of God.

As in the early days of this dispensation, so today those who desire to follow the Chief Shepherd can be cared for and tended by Him, the Shepherd and Overseer of our souls and also by the under-shepherds of the Flock. When the Chief Shepherd appears then those who have faithfully tended the Flock shall rejoice and lay down their burdens of responsibility, whilst those who have been in subjection to Him and to them shall rejoice together. Then "the Lamb which is in the midst of the throne shall be their Shepherd, and shall guide them unto fountains of water of life: and God shall wipe away every tear from their eyes" (Revelation 7:17).

Soon, as Chief Shepherd,

He will come His loved ones home to take,

When those who've served shall have reward,

Who wrought for His name's sake.

Crowned King of Glory then He'll be,

And Lord of Hosts beside,

For Him the heads of lasting doors

And gates will open wide.

The Shepherd thus, Good, Great and Chief,

By cross, and crook, and crown,

Salvation threefold will have wrought

For those He calls His own.

Our God, we're longing for that day

To see the Shepherd King,

Who, with all gathered saints at home,

Will lead the song they sing.

# CHAPTER TWENTY-SIX: THE CORNERSTONE (RICE HORNE)

---

It is recorded of Jacob in Genesis 28 that on the night when he arrived at a certain place "he took one of the stones of the place, and put it under his head, and lay down in that place to sleep"; and that in the morning, he "took the stone that he had put under his head, and set it up for a pillar," saying, "This stone, which I have set up for a pillar, shall be God's house," and so forth. In later scriptures the stone is the figure, or title, which is used to set forth the Lord Jesus in connection with both the Kingdom and the House of God. Nebuchadnezzar in his dream, as recorded in Daniel 2:84, saw:

> "a stone was cut out without hands, which struck the image on its feet of iron and clay, and broke them in pieces. Then the iron, the clay, the bronze, the silver, and the gold were crushed together, and became like chaff from the summer threshing floors; the wind carried them away so that no trace of them was found. And the stone that struck the image became a great mountain and filled the whole earth."

The description of this same blessed One as given through John in Revelation 19:11-16 is thus recorded:

> "Now I saw heaven opened, and behold, a white horse. And He who sat on him was called Faithful and True, and in righteousness He judges and makes war ... His name is called The Word of God ... Now out of His mouth goes a sharpsword, that with it He should strike the nations. And He Himself will rule them with a rod of iron. He Himself

treads the winepress of the fierceness and wrath of Almighty God. And He has on His robe and on His thigh a name written: KING OF KINGS AND LORD OF LORDS."

"The Stone" here is the imagery used to set forth God's King in all His power and majesty as He shall be revealed in a future day. He is the Stone who shall smite the image of Daniel 2 which depicts the combined power and strength of the great Gentile confederacy of nations developed to the full height of attainment to which the ingenuity of man with all his scientific knowledge, and the united wealth of the nations, backed by the power and wisdom of the god of this age, is capable of bringing it. As the Stone shall fall upon the image, it shall be "broken in pieces together," and become like the chaff of the summer threshing floors; and the wind shall carry them away, that no place shall be found for them; and the Stone that smote the image shall become a great Mountain, and fill the whole earth. The glory and might of the nations, He will lay low. "All the nations are as nothing before Him; they are counted to Him less than nothing, and vanity" (Isaiah 40:17).

This same glorious Person is the One of whom the LORD says in Isaiah 28:16, "Behold, I lay in Zion a stone for a foundation, a tried stone, a precious cornerstone of sure foundation" (1 Peter 2:6). Concerning this One the word of the Lord through Peter comes to those who have tasted that the Lord is gracious, "coming to Him as a living stone ... you also as living stones are being built up a spiritual house." Those who Jacob-like have pillowed their head upon the Stone and found peace and rest in Him, having responded to His gracious entreaty, "Come unto Me ... and I will give you rest," are now rejoicing in the truth of the words of the hymn:

Thou Holy One of God,

The Father rests in Thee;

And in the virtue of that blood

Which speaks to Him for me,

The curse is gone; through Thee I'm blest;

God rests in Thee; in Thee I rest.

The foundation Stone is described by the LORD in Isaiah 28:16 as a "tried stone," suggestive of the testing time through which the Lord Jesus passed when He trod this scene, the wilderness temptations through which He came unscathed, the sufferings of His lifetime in which "He learned obedience" and so was "made perfect," - His obedience "even unto death, yea, the death of the cross." Having endured every test, and triumphed over them all, He "sat down on the right hand of the Majesty on high." So He is set forth as the One who is worthy of absolute confidence. The One who having been subjected to every test and having endured, is now presented as the "Stone of SURE foundation." Those who as living stones come to Him to be built into God's house "shall not be put to shame."

The "tried stone" or "stone of proof" also brings Him before us as the "stone of testing" for those who are built into this spiritual house. They must be of such material and shaped in such a manner as to fit into the structure in which He is the chief Corner-Stone. Something of the virtues and character of the Lord Jesus must be generated in those who as living stones are built up a spiritual house. Hence the injunction of 1 Peter 2:1, to put away the un-Christlike traits of character there mentioned. The Spirit of God enjoins upon God's gathered together people the necessity to "put off the old man with his doings" and to "put on the new man." Character and behaviour must be brought into line with the privileged position which is occupied by those who form a house for God to dwell in. How blessedly true are the words of the hymn-writer: "O God, what perfect rest is Thine, Thy rest is in Thy Son."

In Him God found a place of perfect rest. His absolute conformity to God's will, the ever-present desire of His heart to do those things that were pleasing in God's sight; His meditation in God's law day and night; the laying up of God's word in His heart; the unbroken communion which existed between Him and His God, all combined to provide God with a place of perfect rest in Him who is His Son.

He is further described as a "precious" cornerstone, precious surely because of His own intrinsic value. He is the One "in whom are all the treasures of wisdom and knowledge hidden"; "the effulgence of God's glory, and the very image of His substance"; the One in whom God's delight is; the holy, guileless, undefiled One; the chiefest among the ten thousand; the altogether lovely One.

What a wondrous privilege to come to Him and be built into the spiritual house of which He is the Foundation, the chief Cornerstone! How sad that it is recorded of some that they rejected the Stone, and He became to them, "a stone of stumbling." This was the result of disobedience to the word (1 Peter 2:8). If we are to know and enjoy the privileges of those who are in God's house, it can only be as we are obedient to God's word. The "if" of Hebrews 3:6 further emphasizes the conditional character of the house of God.

The desire of the Lord in bringing His people thus together is expressed in the words, "Let them make Me a sanctuary; that I may dwell among them." If this blessed experience is to be enjoyed by God's people, it will be necessary for them to listen to His further word, "What manner of house will ye build unto Me?" and "What place shall be My rest?"

As it was with God's ancient people, so it is with His people today. If God is to have a house to dwell in among them, they must build that house "according to the pattern." When born-again, baptised and added together companies of God's people are seen acting for God as in Acts 2:41 and onwards; each such company is called God's building (1 Corinthians 3:9) or the church of God in the town or city; and to such a company God says, "Ye are temple of God, and the Spirit of God dwelleth in you" (1 Corinthians 4:16. RV). These buildings are again mentioned in Ephesians 2:20-22 (RV), "Each several building, fitly framed together, groweth into a holy temple in the Lord"; the grand purpose of being builded together is that they may be "a habitation of God in the Spirit." Thus the pattern of God's house for this our day is revealed to us, and well it is if we are found, by God's grace, building according to it.

How necessary it is that God's people should be right doctrinally, and how equally important that we should also be right as to our character and behaviour! How solemn were the words of the Lord Jesus to those who had occupied the position of God's testimony in a past day "The kingdom of God shall be taken away from you, and shall be given to a nation bringing forth the fruits thereof"! God had looked for fruit and had been disappointed. Then when the Lord came, the result was as the scripture had predicted, they cast Him out of the vineyard and He became "The Stone which the builders rejected" (Matthew 21:42).

The question was one of fruit. From Israel the fruit was not forth-coming. The honoured place which God had given them was held in high esteem by them, but God was not given that which should have been His from His people. May it be brought home to us who are graced of God to find a place in the nation to which the kingdom of God has been given, that it is expected of us that there shall be the "bringing forth the fruits thereof."

May we, God's people in this day, be exercised before Him to see that He shall receive from us the fruit for which He looks. This can only be as we as individuals know the blessed experience of Christ being formed in us, as we, "with unveiled face reflecting as a mirror the glory of the Lord, are transformed into the same image from glory to glory" (2 Corinthians 3:18).

The high ways we have traversed,

And come to Zion's hill,

Where God, our God, is with us

His purpose to fulfil.

Here are God's house and altar

The place of His great name

Where praise to Him ascendeth

Where we His grace acclaim.

This house for God to dwell in

Of ransome saints is built,

Who by the great atonement

Are purged and free from guilt.

We come to Christ, the Chosen

(The living stone is He)

Through Him to God the Father

To make sweet melody.

# CHAPTER TWENTY-SEVEN: IMMANUEL AND THE SEED OF THE WOMAN (JOHN DRAIN)

The Deity of the Lord Jesus Christ is a truth of very great importance. If Christ is not God the Son, One of full Deity, then the basis on which rests the revelation of God to mankind is destroyed. In the revelation of God contained in the Old Testament Scriptures, there are many indications that One would come who would be the great Deliverer, the King-Messiah. When Adam sinned in Eden he brought far-reaching serious consequences to himself and to the race of which he was head. Sin separates from God and sin brings divine judgement. Sin brought man into bondage and into the power of Satan. In amazing mercy towards mankind the Lord God promised in Eden that One would come who would effectively deal with the powerful enemy who had brought about man's fall.

The promise is contained in the words, "I will put enmity between you and the woman, and between your seed and her seed: he shall bruise your head, and you shall bruise His heel" (Genesis 3:15). From Eden onwards the unfolding of divine purpose saw many references to this coming One. Satan, whose evil workings led to the downfall of Adam, is a very powerful being. But he is a created being. The One whom the Lord God promised - the great Deliverer - is not a created being. True, He was indicated as being the Seed of the woman but He was not the seed of the woman as any other child born by natural generation is the seed of his mother.

The great prophet Isaiah was moved by the Holy Spirit to write concerning the promised One, "Behold, a virgin shall conceive, and bear a Son, and shall call His name Immanuel" (Isaiah 7:14). The Revised Version margin gives the meaning of Immanuel, "God is with us". This Child was to be the virgin's Son, and was to be Immanuel. Later Isaiah wrote, "Unto us a Child is born, unto us a Son is given; and the government shall be upon His shoulder; and His name shall be called Wonderful, Counsellor, Mighty God, Everlasting Father, Prince of Peace" (Isaiah 9:6). To no ordinary child could the words be applied, "Mighty God, Everlasting Father". Where is the Child to whom these profound words are applicable?

In Matthew chapter 1, we read of a virgin who was found to be with child. To allay the fears of the man to whom she was betrothed an angelic messenger was sent to him with the message:

> "She will bring forth a Son; and you shall call His name JESUS". Heaven knew about this Child. "So all this was done that it might be fulfilled which was spoken by the Lord through the prophet, saying:"Behold, the virgin shall be with child, and bear a Son, and they shall call His name Immanuel," which is translated, "God with us" (Matthew 1:22,23).

It is true that God, because of who He is, is omnipresent in the vast universe which He created. But when at Bethlehem the Babe was born to Mary, God, in a manner unique and therefore unprecedented, was with men and women on the earth. The eternal Word, God the Son, "became flesh, and dwelt among us" (John 1:14). The Babe who lay in the manger was Mary's Child, miraculously conceived within her by the power of the Holy Spirit, and He was the Son of God. Here is the great Mystery of God, here is One in whom are full Deity and perfect humanity, two natures in one wondrous Person.

Writing about the coming of Christ into the world Paul said, "When the fulness of the time had come, God sent forth His Son, born of a woman, born under the law ..." (Galatians 4:4). It was the Son whom God the Father sent. He did not send one to be the Son. The Son was with the Father through eternal ages. The time came when the Father sanctified the Son and sent Him into the world. Frequently in His teaching the Lord Jesus claimed that He was the One sent by the Father. It is clear that not merely was pre-existence indicated but also co-equality. The sent One was the Son. The Son was equal with the Father. On one occasion the Lord Jesus said to His opponents, "My Father works even until now, and I work". The Jews immediately grasped the significance of these words. They sought to kill Him "because He not only broke the sabbath, but also called God His own Father, making Himself equal with God". Christ did not contradict this.

Testimony to the truth that Christ was the One sent by the Father was testimony to His Deity. When speaking to the Jews on the occasion referred to in John chapter 5 the Lord pointed out that witness given by Himself might be rejected as unacceptable. But there were other witnesses. John the Baptist, the miraculous works which the Father gave to Christ to accomplish, the Father Himself and the Scriptures, with a particular emphasis on what Moses wrote, all bore testimony to Christ (see John 5:31-46).

When Christ was on the earth He met widespread rejection. Satan mustered his forces of demons and men in opposition. It is very remarkable that though the world knew Him not, demons, who had taken possession of human victims, recognized him. On one occasion there was in the synagogue at Capernaum a man who had a spirit of an unclean demon. When he saw the Lord he cried, "Let us alone! What have we to do with You, Jesus of Nazareth? Did you come to destroy us? I know who You are, the Holy One of God" (Luke 4:34). The demon saw more than the humble Man of Nazareth. He saw the Holy One of God.

On another occasion when the Lord was speaking to His disciples He brought up the matter of His identity. He questioned the disciples as to the opinions of the people generally. Then He asked, "But who do you say that I am?" From Peter came the answer, "You are the Christ, the Son of the living God" (Matthew 16:16). Others had said John the Baptist, Elijah, Jeremiah. These certainly were great men. But Jesus was not just a great man on a plane comparable with those men who were cited. He was the Christ, the Son of the living God. Great words and great works mark a man as being great in the eyes of his fellows. Something more was involved in Peter's confession. Said the Lord, "Blessed are you, Simon Bar-Jonah: for flesh and blood has not revealed this to you, but My Father who is in heaven" (Matthew 16:17). Flesh and blood could reveal the identity of a great man. Divine revelation and enlightenment were required to bring to Simon Peter that Jesus of Nazareth was the Christ and the Son of God, God the Son.

The historic manifestation of Christ on earth was an important crisis in divine purpose and revelation. It meant that there was a Man on earth who was God the Son. A hymn-writer has expressed this truth in his words,

Yet One from Thee, oh matchless grace

Oh, wondrous mystery divine!

In human form did take man's place,

And God and man in one combine"

When after His death and resurrection Christ ascended to take His place at the right hand of God there was on the throne of God the Man who was God the Son. This great truth held a central place in the mes-

# SPARKLING FACETS: BIBLE NAMES AND TITLES OF JESUS

sage of God to men in a new dispensation which opened up on the day of Pentecost.

The writings of Peter and John show that they believed Jesus to be God the Son. The Christology of Paul, which was in fact the accepted revelation of the Holy Spirit to Paul, is crystal clear in its testimony to the Deity of Christ. Space would not permit an examination of this testimony, but we refer to some of Paul's statements on this matter. When writing to the Romans the apostle said concerning his kinsmen according to the flesh, "who are Israelites, to whom pertain the adoption, the glory, the covenants, the giving of the law, the service of God, and the promises; of whom are the fathers and from whom, according to the flesh, Christ came, who is over all, the eternally blessed God. Amen" (Romans 9:4,5).

To the Philippians Paul said of Christ Jesus, "who, being in the form of God, counted it not a prize to be on an equality with God" (Philippians 2:6). Greek scholars have shown that the expression "form of God" includes the whole nature and essence of Deity. Whatever changes were involved in the Incarnation Christ was essentially God. He never could be anything else. He could empty Himself of many manifestations of the glory and prerogatives which were His as being on an equality with God. But He could not empty Himself of His essential Being, and in His Being He is God.

The saints in the church of God in Colossae were feeling the effects of attacks by the adversary on the Person of Christ. The Spirit of God moved the apostle to write to these saints, and amongst other profound and instructive truths concerning the Lord Jesus Christ we have, "in Him dwells all the fulness of the Godhead bodily" (Colossians 2:9). The fulness of Deity is in Christ. All that God is Christ is. He is of the same nature as God the Father and God the Spirit. To Him belong the same infinite attributes. There can be no doubt that to Paul Jesus of Nazareth was God manifested in the flesh. And as He contemplated the return of Christ Paul wrote, "... looking for the blessed hope and glorious appearing of our great God and Saviour Jesus Christ ..." (Titus 2:13).

The witness of Scripture is clear. Christ is our great God, God the Son, of the full Deity possessed. The confession of His disciples finds its language in the words of Thomas, "My Lord and my God".

Did you love *Sparkling Facets: Bible Names and Titles of Jesus*? Then you should read *Back to Basics: A Guide to Essential Bible Teaching* by Hayes Press!

This book uses a combination of teaching and practical content and study questions to explore 8 key topics that are essential to the Christian faith: Knowing God, Salvation, Believer's Baptism, The Breaking of Bread, Understanding The Bible, The Return of Jesus Christ, Spiritual Gifts, Church Life - Why, what, where? This book contains a section of study questions and is ideal for personal or group Bible study.

# Also by Hayes Press

**Needed Truth**
Needed Truth 1888
Needed Truth 2001
Needed Truth 2002
Needed Truth 2003
Needed Truth 2004
Needed Truth 2005
Needed Truth 2006
Needed Truth 2007
Needed Truth 2008
Needed Truth 2009
Needed Truth 2010
Needed Truth 2011
Needed Truth 2012
Needed Truth 2015
Needed Truth 1888-1988: A Centenary Review of Major Themes

**Standalone**
The Road Through Calvary: 40 Devotional Readings
Lovers of God's House
Different Discipleship: Jesus' Sermon on the Mount
The House of God: Past, Present and Future

The Kingdom of God
Knowing God: His Names and Nature
Churches of God: Their Biblical Constitution and Functions
Four Books About Jesus
Collected Writings On ... Exploring Biblical Fellowship
Collected Writings On ... Exploring Biblical Hope
Collected Writings On ... The Cross of Christ
Builders for God
Collected Writings On ... Exploring Biblical Faithfulness
Collected Writings On ... Exploring Biblical Joy
Possessing the Land: Spiritual Lessons from Joshua
Collected Writings On ... Exploring Biblical Holiness
Collected Writings On ... Exploring Biblical Faith
Collected Writings On ... Exploring Biblical Love
These Three Remain...Exploring Biblical Faith, Hope and Love
The Teaching and Testimony of the Apostles
Pressure Points - Biblical Advice for 20 of Life's Biggest Challenges
More Than a Saviour: Exploring the Person and Work of Jesus
The Psalms: Volumes 1-4 Boxset
The Faith: Outlines of Scripture Doctrine
Key Doctrines of the Christian Gospel
Is There a Purpose to Life?
Bible Covenants 101
The Hidden Christ - Volume 2: Types and Shadows in Offerings and Sacrifices
The Hidden Christ Volume 1: Types and Shadows in the Old Testament
The Hidden Christ - Volume 3: Types and Shadows in Genesis
Heavenly Meanings - The Parables of Jesus
Fisherman to Follower: The Life and Teaching of Simon Peter
Called to Serve: Lessons from the Levites
Needed Truth 2017 Issue 1
The Breaking of the Bread: Its History, Its Observance, Its Meaning

Spiritual Revivals of the Bible
An Introduction to the Book of Hebrews
The Holy Spirit and the Believer
The Psalms: Volume 1 - Thoughts on Key Themes
The Psalms: Volume 2 - Exploring Key Elements
The Psalms: Volume 3 - Surveying Key Sections
The Psalms: Volume 4 - Savouring Choice Selections
Profiles of the Prophets
The Hidden Christ - Volumes 1-4 Box Set
The Hidden Christ - Volume 4: Types and Shadows in Israel's Tabernacle
Baptism - Its Meaning and Teaching
Conflict and Controversy in the Church of God in Corinth
In the Shadow of Calvary: A Bible Study of John 12-17
Moses: God's Deliverer
Sparkling Facets: Bible Names and Titles of Jesus
A Little Book About Being Christlike
Keys to Church Growth
From Shepherd Boy to Sovereign: The Life of David
Back to Basics: A Guide to Essential Bible Teaching
An Introduction to the Holy Spirit
Israel and the Church in Bible Prophecy
"Growth and Fruit" and Other Writings by John Drain
15 Hot Topics For Today's Christian
Needed Truth Volume 2 1889
Studies on the Return of Christ
Studies on the Resurrection of Christ
Needed Truth Volume 3 1890
The Nations of the Old Testament: Their Relationship with Israel and Bible Prophecy
The Message of the Minor Prophets
Insights from Isaiah
The Bible - Its Inspiration and Authority

Lessons from Ezra and Nehemiah
A Bible Study of God's Names For His People

## About the Publisher

Hayes Press (www.hayespress.org) is a registered charity in the United Kingdom, whose primary mission is to disseminate the Word of God, mainly through literature. It is one of the largest distributors of gospel tracts and leaflets in the United Kingdom, with over 100 titles and hundreds of thousands despatched annually. In addition to paperbacks and eBooks, Hayes Press also publishes Plus Eagles Wings, a fun and educational Bible magazine for children, and Golden Bells, a popular daily Bible reading calendar in wall or desk formats. Also available are over 100 Bibles in many different versions, shapes and sizes, Bible text posters and much more!

www.ingramcontent.com/pod-product-compliance
Lightning Source LLC
Chambersburg PA
CBHW031358040426
42444CB00005B/344